A hopeful journey...

On the twenty-sixth, just before we went on the ship, my father sent my grandmother a cablegram: SAILING TODAY. I wanted him to add "Hooray," but every word cost money, he said, and besides she'd recognize the hooray even if it wasn't there. Certainly on board the *President Taft* the hooray feeling was all over the place. On deck the ship's band was playing "California, Here I Come," and people were dancing and singing and laughing. A steward was handing out rolls of paper streamers for passengers to throw over the railing as the ship sailed.

When the whistle blew for visitors to leave, I went to Andrea and stood beside her. Together we threw our streamers as the ship began to pull away from the dock. Everyone threw. Roll after roll until the distance from the ship to the dock was aflutter with paper ribbons—red, yellow, blue, green. Flimsy things, they looked as if they didn't want to let Shanghai go.

It seemed to me that once we were completely out of sight of land, I would really feel homeward bound. But as I looked at the Shanghai skyline and at the busy waterfront, I had the strange feeling that I wasn't moving away at all.

Homesick
my own story

JEAN FRITZ

ILLUSTRATED BY MARGOT TOMES

PUFFIN BOOKS

TO THE MEMORY OF
MY MOTHER AND FATHER

PUFFIN BOOKS
Published by the Penguin Group
Penguin Young Readers Group,
345 Hudson Street, New York, New York 10014, U.S.A.
Penguin Group (Canada), 90 Eglinton Avenue East, Suite 700, Toronto,
Ontario, Canada M4P 2Y3 (a division of Pearson Penguin Canada Inc.)
Penguin Books Ltd, 80 Strand, London WC2R 0RL, England
Penguin Ireland, 25 St Stephen's Green, Dublin 2, Ireland
(a division of Penguin Books Ltd)
Penguin Group (Australia), 250 Camberwell Road, Camberwell,
Victoria 3124, Australia (a division of Pearson Australia Group Pty Ltd)
Penguin Books India Pvt Ltd, 11 Community Centre, Panchsheel Park,
New Delhi - 110 017, India
Penguin Group (NZ), Cnr Airborne and Rosedale Roads, Albany,
Auckland 1310, New Zealand (a division of Pearson New Zealand Ltd)
Penguin Books (South Africa) (Pty) Ltd, 24 Sturdee Avenue,
Rosebank, Johannesburg 2196, South Africa

Registered Offices: Penguin Books Ltd, 80 Strand, London WC2R 0RL, England

First published in the United States of America by G. P. Putnam's Sons, 1982
Published by Penguin Putnam Books for Young Readers, 1999
Published by Puffin Books, a division of Penguin Young Readers Group, 2007

1 3 5 7 9 10 8 6 4 2

THE LIBRARY OF CONGRESS HAS CATALOGED THE G. P. PUTNAM'S SONS EDITION AS FOLLOWS:
Fritz, Jean. Homesick, my own story.
Summary: The author's fictionalized version, though all the events are true, of her
childhood in China in the 1920's.
ISBN: 0-399-20933-6 (hc)
1. Fritz, Jean—Juvenile fiction. (1. Fritz, Jean—Fiction. 2. China—Fiction.)
I. Tomes, Margot, ill. II. Title. PZ7.F919Hn 1982 [Fic] 82-7646

Puffin Books ISBN 978-0-14-240761-5

Printed in the United States of America

PUFFIN MODERN CLASSICS

My special thanks go to Dorothy Bruhl Anderson, who lived in Hankow and who encouraged and helped me to remember. And to Dr. C. Martin Wilbur, an old China friend, who allowed me to draw on his knowledge and understanding.

FOREWORD

When I started to write about my childhood in China, I found that my memory came out in lumps. Although I could for the most part arrange them in the proper sequence, I discovered that my preoccupation with time and literal accuracy was squeezing the life out of what I had to say. So I decided to forget about sequence and just get on with it.

Since my childhood feels like a story, I decided to tell it that way, letting the events fall as they would into the shape of a story, lacing them together with fictional bits, adding a piece here and there when memory didn't give me all I needed. I would use conversation freely, for I cannot think of my childhood without hearing voices. So although this book takes place within two years—from October 1925 to September 1927—the events are drawn from the entire period of my childhood, but they are all, except in minor details, basically true. The people are real people; the places are dear to me. But most important, the form I have used has given me the freedom to recreate the emotions that I remember so vividly. Strictly speaking, I have to call this book *fiction*, but it does not feel like fiction to me. It is my story, told as truly as I can tell it.

JEAN FRITZ

DOBBS FERRY, NEW YORK
JANUARY 11, 1982

1

In my father's study there was a large globe with all the countries of the world running around it. I could put my finger on the exact spot where I was and had been ever since I'd been born. And I was on the wrong side of the globe. I was in China in a city named Hankow, a dot on a crooked line that seemed to break the country right in two. The line was really the Yangtse River, but who would know by looking at a map what the Yangtse River really was?

Orange-brown, muddy mustard-colored. And wide, wide, wide. With a river smell that was old and came all the way up from the bottom. Sometimes old women knelt on the riverbank, begging the River God to return a son or grandson who may have drowned. They would wail and beat the earth to make the River God pay attention, but I knew how busy the River God must be. All those people on the Yangtse River! Coolies hauling water. Women washing clothes. Houseboats swarming with old people and young, chickens and pigs. Big crooked-sailed junks with eyes painted on their prows so they could see where they were going. I loved the Yangtse River, but, of course, I belonged on the other side of the world. In America with my grandmother.

Twenty-five fluffy little yellow chicks hatched from our eggs today, my grandmother wrote.

I wrote my grandmother that I had watched a Chinese magician swallow three yards of fire.

The trouble with living on the wrong side of the world was that I didn't feel like a *real* American.

For instance. I could never be president of the United States. I didn't want to be president; I wanted to be a writer. Still, why should there be a *law* saying that only a person born in the United States could be president? It was as if I wouldn't be American enough.

Actually, I was American every minute of the day, especially during school hours. I went to a British school and every morning we sang "God Save the King." Of course the British children loved singing about their gracious king. Ian Forbes stuck out his chest and sang as if he were saving the king all by himself. Everyone sang. Even Gina Boss who was Italian. And Vera Sebastian who was so Russian she dressed the way Russian girls did long ago before the Revolution when her family had to run away to keep from being killed.

But I wasn't Vera Sebastian. I asked my mother to write an excuse so I wouldn't have to sing, but she wouldn't do it. "When in Rome," she said, "do as the Romans do." What she meant was, "Don't make trouble. Just sing." So for a long time I did. I sang with my fingers crossed but still I felt like a traitor.

Then one day I thought: If my mother and father were really and truly in Rome, they wouldn't do what the Romans did at all. They'd probably try to get the Romans to do what *they* did, just as they were trying to teach the Chinese to do what Americans did. (My mother even gave classes in American manners.)

So that day I quit singing. I kept my mouth locked tight against the king of England. Our teacher, Miss Williams, didn't notice at first. She stood in front of the room, using a ruler for a baton, striking each syllable so hard it was as if she were making up for the times she had nothing to strike.

(Miss Williams was pinch-faced and bossy. Sometimes I wondered what had ever made her come to China. "Maybe to try and catch a husband," my mother said.

A husband! Miss Williams!)

"Make him vic-tor-i-ous," the class sang. It was on the strike of "vic" that Miss Williams noticed. Her eyes lighted on my mouth and when we sat down, she pointed her ruler at me.

"Is there something wrong with your voice today, Jean?" she asked.

"No, Miss Williams."

"You weren't singing."

"No, Miss Williams. It is not my national anthem."

"It is the national anthem we sing here," she snapped. "You have always sung. Even Vera sings it."

I looked at Vera with the big blue bow tied on the top of her head. Usually I felt sorry for her but not today. At recess I might even untie that bow, I thought. Just give it a yank. But if I'd been smart, I wouldn't have been looking at Vera. I would have been looking at Ian Forbes and I would have known that, no matter what Miss Williams said, I wasn't through with the king of England.

Recess at the British School was nothing I looked forward to. Every day we played a game called prisoner's base, which was all running and shouting and shoving and catching. I hated the game, yet everyone played except Vera Sebastian. She sat on the sidelines under her blue bow like someone who had been dropped out of a history book. By recess I had forgotten my plans for that bow. While everyone was getting ready for the game, I was as usual trying to look as if I didn't care if I was the last one picked for a team or not. I was leaning against the high stone wall that ran around the school-yard. I was looking up at a little white cloud skittering across the sky when all at once someone tramped down hard on my right foot. Ian Forbes. Snarling bulldog face. Heel grinding down on my toes. Head thrust forward the way an animal might before it strikes.

"You wouldn't sing it. So say it," he ordered. "Let me hear you say it."

I tried to pull my foot away but he only ground down harder.

"Say what?" I was telling my face please not to show what my foot felt.

"*God save the king*. Say it. Those four words. I want to hear you say it."

Although Ian Forbes was short, he was solid and tough and built for fighting. What was more, he always won. You had only to look at his bare knees between the top of his socks and his short pants to know that he would win. His knees were square. Bony and unbeatable. So of course it was crazy for me to argue with him.

"Why should I?" I asked. "Americans haven't said that since George the Third."

He grabbed my right arm and twisted it behind my back.

"Say it," he hissed.

I felt the tears come to my eyes and I hated myself for the tears. I hated myself for not staying in Rome the way my mother had told me.

"I'll never say it," I whispered.

They were choosing sides now in the schoolyard and Ian's name was being called—among the first as always.

He gave my arm another twist. "You'll sing tomorrow," he snarled, "or you'll be bloody sorry."

As he ran off, I slid to the ground, my head between my knees.

Oh, Grandma, I thought, why can't I be there with you? I'd feed the chickens for you. I'd pump water from the well, the way my father used to do.

It would be almost two years before we'd go to America. I was ten years old now; I'd be twelve then. But how could I think about *years*? I didn't even dare to think about the next day. After school I ran all the way home, fast so I couldn't think at all.

Our house stood behind a high stone wall which had chips of broken glass sticking up from the top to keep thieves away. I flung open the iron gate and threw myself through the front door.

"I'm home!" I yelled.

Then I remembered that it was Tuesday, the day my mother taught an English class at the Y.M.C.A. where my father was the director.

I stood in the hall, trying to catch my breath, and as always I began to feel small. It was a huge hall with ceilings so high it was as if they would have nothing to do with people. Certainly not with a mere child, not with me—the only child in the house. Once I asked my best friend, Andrea, if the hall made her feel little too. She said no. She was going to be a dancer and she loved space. She did a high kick to show how grand it was to have room.

Andrea Hull was a year older than I was and knew about everything sooner. She told me about commas,

for instance, long before I took punctuation seriously.
How could I write letters without commas? she asked.
She made me so ashamed that for months I hung little
wagging comma-tails all over the letters to my grandmother. She told me things that sounded so crazy I had
to ask my mother if they were true. Like where babies
came from. And that someday the whole world would
end. My mother would frown when I asked her, but she
always agreed that Andrea was right. It made me
furious. How could she know such things and not tell
me? What was the matter with grown-ups anyway?

I wished that Andrea were with me now, but she
lived out in the country and I didn't see her often. Lin
Nai-Nai, my amah, was the only one around, and of
course I knew she'd be there. It was her job to stay with
me when my parents were out. As soon as she heard me
come in, she'd called, "Tsai loushang," which meant
that she was upstairs. She might be mending or ironing
but most likely she'd be sitting by the window embroi-
dering. And she was. She even had my embroidery laid
out, for we had made a bargain. She would teach me to
embroider if I would teach her English. I liked embroi-
dering: the cloth stretched tight within my embroidery
hoop while I filled in the stamped pattern with cross-
stitches and lazy daisy flowers. The trouble was that
lazy daisies needed French knots for their centers and I
hated making French knots. Mine always fell apart, so I
left them to the end. Today I had twenty lazy daisies
waiting for their knots.

Lin Nai-Nai had already threaded my needle with
embroidery floss.

"Black centers," she said, "for the yellow flowers."

I felt myself glowering. "American flowers don't
have centers," I said and gave her back the needle.

Lin Nai-Nai looked at me, puzzled, but she did not

argue. She was different from other amahs. She did not even come from the servant class, although this was a secret we had to keep from the other servants who would have made her life miserable, had they known. She had run away from her husband when he had taken a second wife. She would always have been Wife Number One and the Boss no matter how many wives he had, but she would rather be no wife than head of a string of wives. She was modern. She might look old-fashioned, for her feet had been bound up tight when she was a little girl so that they would stay small, and now, like many Chinese women, she walked around on little stumps stuffed into tiny cloth shoes. Lin Nai-Nai's were embroidered with butterflies. Still, she believed in true love and one wife for one husband. We were good friends, Lin Nai-Nai and I, so I didn't know why I felt so mean.

She shrugged. "English lesson?" she asked, smiling.

I tested my arm to see if it still hurt from the twisting. It did. My foot too. "What do you want to know?" I asked.

We had been through the polite phrases—Please, Thank you, I beg your pardon, Excuse me, You're welcome, Merry Christmas (which she had practiced but hadn't had a chance to use since this was only October).

"If I meet an American on the street," she asked, "how do I greet him?"

I looked her straight in the eye and nodded my head in a greeting. "Sewing machine," I said. "You say, 'Sew-ing ma-chine.'"

She repeated after me, making the four syllables into four separate words. She got up and walked across the room, bowing and smiling. "Sew Ing Ma Shing."

Part of me wanted to laugh at the thought of Lin Nai-Nai maybe meeting Dr. Carhart, our minister, whose face would surely puff up, the way it always did when he was flustered. But part of me didn't want to laugh at all. I didn't like it when my feelings got tangled, so I ran downstairs and played chopsticks on the piano. Loud and fast. When my sore arm hurt, I just beat on the keys harder.

Then I went out to the kitchen to see if Yang Sze-Fu, the cook, would give me something to eat. I found him reading a Chinese newspaper, his eyes going up and down with the characters. (Chinese words don't march across flat surfaces the way ours do; they drop down cliffs, one cliff after another from right to left across a page.)

"Can I have a piece of cinnamon toast?" I asked. "And a cup of cocoa?"

Yang Sze-Fu grunted. He was smoking a cigarette, which he wasn't supposed to do in the kitchen, but Yang Sze-Fu mostly did what he wanted. He considered himself superior to common workers. You could tell because of the fingernails on his pinkies. They were at least two inches long, which was his way of showing that he didn't have to use his hands for rough or dirty work. He didn't seem to care that his fingernails were dirty, but maybe he couldn't keep such long nails clean.

He made my toast while his cigarette dangled out of the corner of his mouth, collecting a long ash that finally fell on the floor. He wouldn't have kept smoking if my mother had been there, although he didn't always pay attention to my mother. Never about butter pagodas, for instance. No matter how many times my mother told him before a dinner party, "No butter pagoda," it made no difference. As soon as everyone was seated, the serving boy, Wong Sze-Fu, would bring in a pagoda and set it on the table. The guests would "oh" and "ah," for it was a masterpiece: a pagoda molded out of butter, curved roofs rising tier upon tier, but my mother could only think how unsanitary it was. For, of course, Yang Sze-Fu had molded the butter with his hands and carved the decorations with one of his long fingernails. Still, we always used the butter, for if my mother sent it back to the kitchen, Yang Sze-Fu would lose face and quit.

When my toast and cocoa were ready, I took them upstairs to my room (the blue room) and while I ate, I began *Sara Crewe* again. Now there was a girl, I thought, who was worth crying over. I wasn't going to think about myself. Or Ian Forbes. Or the next day. I wasn't. I wasn't.

And I didn't. Not all afternoon. Not all evening. Still, I must have decided what I was going to do because the next morning when I started for school and came to the corner where the man sold hot chestnuts, the corner where I always turned to go to school, I didn't turn. I walked straight ahead. I wasn't going to school that day.

I walked toward the Yangtse River. Past the store that sold paper pellets that opened up into flowers when you dropped them in a glass of water. Then up the block where the beggars sat. I never saw anyone give money to a beggar. You couldn't, my father explained, or you'd be mobbed by beggars. They'd follow you everyplace; they'd never leave you alone. I had learned not to look at them when I passed and yet I saw. The running sores, the twisted legs, the mangled faces. What I couldn't get over was that, like me, each one of those beggars had only one life to live. It just happened that they had drawn rotten ones.

Oh, Grandma, I thought, we may be far apart but we're lucky, you and I. Do you even know how lucky? In America do you know?

This part of the city didn't actually belong to the Chinese, even though the beggars sat there, even though upper-class Chinese lived there. A long time ago other countries had just walked into China and divided up part of Hankow (and other cities) into sections, or concessions, which they called their own and used their own rules for governing. We lived in the French concession on Rue de Paris. Then there was the British concession and the Japanese. The Russian and German concessions had been officially returned to China, but the people still called them concessions. The Americans didn't have one, although, like some of the other countries, they had gunboats on the river. In case, my father said. In case what? Just in case. That's all he'd say.

The concessions didn't look like the rest of China. The buildings were solemn and orderly with little plots of grass around them. Not like those in the Chinese part of the city: a jumble of rickety shops with people, vegetables, crates of quacking ducks, yard goods, bamboo baskets, and mangy dogs spilling onto a street so narrow it was hardly there.

The grandest street in Hankow was the Bund, which ran along beside the Yangtse River. When I came to it after passing the beggars, I looked to my left and saw the American flag flying over the American consulate building. I was proud of the flag and I thought maybe today it was proud of me. It flapped in the breeze as if it were saying ha-ha to the king of England.

Then I looked to the right at the Customs House,

which stood at the other end of the Bund. The clock on top of the tower said nine-thirty. How would I spend the day?

I crossed the street to the promenade part of the Bund. When people walked here, they weren't usually going anyplace; they were just out for the air. My mother would wear her broad-brimmed beaver hat when we came and my father would swing his cane in that jaunty way that showed how glad he was to be a man. I thought I would just sit on a bench for the morning. I would watch the Customs House clock, and when it was time, I would eat the lunch I had brought along in my schoolbag.

I was the only one sitting on a bench. People did not generally "take the air" on a Wednesday morning and besides, not everyone was allowed here. The British had put a sign on the Bund, NO DOGS, NO CHINESE. This meant that I could never bring Lin Nai-Nai with me. My father couldn't even bring his best friend, Mr. T. K. Hu. Maybe the British wanted a place where they could pretend they weren't in China, I thought. Still, there were always Chinese coolies around. In order to load and unload boats in the river, coolies had to cross the Bund. All day they went back and forth, bent double under their loads, sweating and chanting in a tired, singsong way that seemed to get them from one step to the next.

To pass the time, I decided to recite poetry. The one good thing about Miss Williams was that she made us learn poems by heart and I liked that. There was one particular poem I didn't want to forget. I looked at the Yangtse River and pretended that all the busy people in the boats were my audience.

" 'Breathes there the man, with soul so dead,' " I

cried, " 'Who never to himself hath said, This is my own, my native land!'"

I was so carried away by my performance that I didn't notice the policeman until he was right in front of me. Like all policemen in the British concession, he was a bushy-bearded Indian with a red turban wrapped around his head.

He pointed to my schoolbag. "Little miss," he said, "why aren't you in school?"

He was tall and mysterious-looking, more like a character in my Arabian Nights book than a man you expected to talk to. I fumbled for an answer. "I'm going on an errand," I said finally. "I just sat down for a rest." I picked up my schoolbag and walked quickly away. When I looked around, he was back on his corner, directing traffic.

So now they were chasing children away too, I thought angrily. Well, I'd like to show them. Someday I'd like to walk a dog down the whole length of the Bund. A Great Dane. I'd have him on a leash—like this—(I put out my hand as if I were holding a leash right then) and he'd be so big and strong I'd have to strain to hold him back (I strained). Then of course sometimes he'd have to do his business and I'd stop (like this) right in the middle of the sidewalk and let him go to it. I was so busy with my Great Dane I was at the end of the Bund before I knew it. I let go of the leash, clapped my hands, and told my dog to go home. Then I left the Bund and the concessions and walked into the Chinese world.

My mother and father and I had walked here but not for many months. This part near the river was called the Mud Flats. Sometimes it was muddier than others, and when the river flooded, the flats disappeared underwater. Sometimes even the fishermen's huts were washed away, knocked right off their long-legged stilts and swept down the river. But today the river was fairly low and the mud had dried so that it was cracked and cakey. Most of the men who lived here were out fishing, some not far from the shore, poling their sampans through the shallow water. Only a few people were on the flats: a man cleaning fish on a flat rock at the water's edge, a woman spreading clothes on the dirt to dry, a few small children. But behind the huts was something I had never seen before. Even before I came close, I guessed what it was. Even then, I was excited by the strangeness of it.

It was the beginnings of a boat. The skeleton of a large junk, its ribs lying bare, its backbone running straight and true down the bottom. The outline of the prow was already in place, turning up wide and snub-nosed, the way all junks did. I had never thought of boats starting from nothing, of taking on bones under their bodies. The eyes, I supposed, would be the last thing added. Then the junk would have life.

The builders were not there and I was behind the huts where no one could see me as I walked around and around, marveling. Then I climbed inside and as I did, I knew that something wonderful was happening to me. I was a-tingle, the way a magician must feel when he swallows fire, because suddenly I knew that the boat was mine. No matter who really owned it, it was mine. Even if I never saw it again, it would be my junk sailing up and down the Yangtse River. My junk seeing the river sights with its two eyes, seeing them for me whether I was there or not. Often I had tried to put the Yangtse River into a poem so I could keep it. Sometimes I had tried to draw it, but nothing I did ever came close. But now, *now* I had my junk and somehow that gave me the river too.

I thought I should put my mark on the boat. Perhaps on the side of the spine. Very small. A secret between the boat and me. I opened my schoolbag and took out my folding penknife that I used for sharpening pencils. Very carefully I carved the Chinese character that was our name. Gau. (In China my father was Mr. Gau, my mother was Mrs. Gau, and I was Little Miss Gau.) The builders would paint right over the character, I thought, and never notice. But I would know. Always and forever I would know.

For a long time I dreamed about the boat, imagining it finished, its sails up, its eyes wide. Someday it might sail all the way down the Yangtse to Shanghai, so I told the boat what it would see along the way because I had been there and the boat hadn't. After a while I got hungry and I ate my egg sandwich. I was in the midst of peeling an orange when all at once I had company.

A small boy, not more than four years old, wandered around to the back of the huts, saw me, and stopped still. He was wearing a ragged blue cotton jacket with a red cloth, pincushion-like charm around his neck which was supposed to keep him from getting smallpox. Sticking up straight from the middle of his head was a small pigtail which I knew was to fool the gods and make them think he was a girl. (Gods didn't bother much with girls; it was boys that were important in China.) The weather was still warm so he wore no pants, nothing below the waist. Most small boys went around like this so that when they had to go, they could just let loose and go. He walked slowly up to the boat, stared at me, and then nodded as if he'd already guessed what I was. "Foreign devil," he announced gravely.

I shook my head. "No," I said in Chinese. "American friend." Through the ribs of the boat, I handed him a segment of orange. He ate it slowly, his eyes on the rest of the orange. Segment by segment, I gave it all to him. Then he wiped his hands down the front of his jacket.

"Foreign devil," he repeated.

"American friend," I corrected. Then I asked him about the boat. Who was building it? Where were the builders?

He pointed with his chin upriver. "Not here today. Back tomorrow."

I knew it would only be a question of time before the boy would run off to alert the people in the huts. "Foreign devil, foreign devil," he would cry. So I put my hand on the prow of the boat, wished it luck, and climbing out, I started back toward the Bund. To my surprise the boy walked beside me. When we came to the edge of the Bund, I squatted down so we would be on the same eye level.

"Good-bye," I said. "May the River God protect you."

For a moment the boy stared. When he spoke, it was as if he were trying out a new sound. "American friend," he said slowly.

When I looked back, he was still there, looking soberly toward the foreign world to which I had gone.

The time, according to the Customs House clock, was five after two, which meant that I couldn't go home for two hours. School was dismissed at three-thirty and I was home by three-forty-five unless I had to stay in for talking in class. It took me about fifteen minutes to write "I will not talk in class" fifty times, and so I often came home at four o'clock. (I wrote up and down like the Chinese: fifty "I's," fifty "wills," and right through the sentence so I never had to think what I was writing. It wasn't as if I were making a promise.) Today I planned to arrive home at four, my "staying-in" time, in the hope that I wouldn't meet classmates on the way.

Meanwhile I wandered up and down the streets, in and out of stores. I weighed myself on the big scale in the Hankow Dispensary and found that I was as skinny as ever. I went to the Terminus Hotel and tried out the chairs in the lounge. At first I didn't mind wandering about like this. Half of my mind was still on the river with my junk, but as time went on, my junk began slipping away until I was alone with nothing but questions. Would my mother find out about today? How could I skip school tomorrow? And the next day and the next? Could I get sick? Was there a kind of long lie-abed sickness that didn't hurt?

I arrived home at four, just as I had planned, opened the door, and called out, "I'm home!" Cheery-like and normal. But I was scarcely in the house before Lin Nai-Nai ran to me from one side of the hall and my mother from the other.

"Are you all right? Are you all right?" Lin Nai-Nai felt my arms as if she expected them to be broken. My mother's face was white. "What happened?" she asked.

Then I looked through the open door into the living room and saw Miss Williams sitting there. She had beaten me home and asked about my absence, which of course had scared everyone. But now my mother could see that I was in one piece and for some reason this seemed to make her mad. She took me by the hand and led me into the living room. "Miss Williams said you weren't in school," she said. "Why was that?"

I hung my head, just the way cowards do in books.

My mother dropped my hand. "Jean will be in school tomorrow," she said firmly. She walked Miss Williams to the door. "Thank you for stopping by."

Miss Williams looked satisfied in her mean, pinched way. "Well," she said, "ta-ta." (She always said "ta-ta" instead of "good-bye." Chicken language, it sounded like.)

As soon as Miss Williams was gone and my mother was sitting down again, I burst into tears. Kneeling on the floor, I buried my head in her lap and poured out the whole miserable story. My mother could see that I really wasn't in one piece after all, so she listened quietly, stroking my hair as I talked, but gradually I could feel her stiffen. I knew she was remembering that she was a Mother.

"You better go up to your room," she said, "and think things over. We'll talk about it after supper."

I flung myself on my bed. What was there to think? Either I went to school and got beaten up. Or I quit.

After supper I explained to my mother and father how simple it was. I could stay at home and my mother could teach me, the way Andrea's mother taught her. Maybe I could even go to Andrea's house and study with her.

My mother shook her head. Yes, it was simple, she agreed. I could go back to the British School, be sensible, and start singing about the king again.

I clutched the edge of the table. Couldn't she understand? I couldn't turn back now. It was too late.

So far my father had not said a word. He was leaning back, teetering on the two hind legs of his chair, the way he always did after a meal, the way that drove my mother crazy. But he was not the kind of person to keep all four legs of a chair on the floor just because someone wanted him to. He wasn't a turning-back person so I hoped maybe he would understand. As I watched him, I saw a twinkle start in his eyes and suddenly he brought his chair down slam-bang flat on the floor. He got up and motioned for us to follow him into the living room. He sat down at the piano and began to pick out the tune for "God Save the King."

A big help, I thought. Was he going to make me practice?

Then he began to sing:

"My country 'tis of thee,

Sweet land of liberty, . . ."

Of course! It was the same tune. Why hadn't I thought of that? Who would know what I was singing as long as I moved my lips? I joined in now, loud and strong.

"Of thee I sing."

My mother laughed in spite of herself. "If you sing that loud," she said, "you'll start a revolution."

"Tomorrow I'll sing softly," I promised. "No one will know." But for now I really let freedom ring.

Then all at once I wanted to see Lin Nai-Nai. I ran out back, through the courtyard that separated the house from the servants' quarters, and upstairs to her room.

"It's me," I called through the door and when she opened up, I threw my arms around her. "Oh, Lin Nai-Nai, I love you," I said. "You haven't said it yet, have you?"

"Said what?"

"Sewing machine. You haven't said it?"

"No," she said, "not yet. I'm still practicing."

"Don't say it, Lin Nai-Nai. Say 'Good day.' It's shorter and easier. Besides, it's more polite."

"Good day?" she repeated.

"Yes, that's right. Good day." I hugged her and ran back to the house.

The next day at school when we rose to sing the British national anthem, everyone stared at me, but as soon as I opened my mouth, the class lost interest. All but Ian Forbes. His eyes never left my face, but I sang softly, carefully, proudly. At recess he sauntered over to where I stood against the wall.

He spat on the ground. "You can be bloody glad you sang today," he said. Then he strutted off as if he and those square knees of his had won again.

And, of course, I was bloody glad.

2

I ALWAYS THOUGHT I WOULD FEEL MORE AMERI-
can if I'd been named Marjorie. I could picture a girl
named Marjorie roller skating in America (I had never
roller-skated). Or sled riding (there was neither snow
nor hills in Hankow). Or being wild on Halloween
night (I had never celebrated Halloween). The name
Jean was so short, there didn't seem to be enough room
in it for all the things I wanted to do, all the ways I
wanted to be. Sometimes I wondered if my mother had
picked a short name because she had her heart set on
my being just one kind of person. Ever since she'd written in my autograph book, I was afraid that goodness
was what she really wanted out of me.

"Be good, sweet child," she had written, "and let
who will be clever."

Deep in my heart I knew that goodness didn't come
natural to me. If I had to choose, I would rather be
clever, but I didn't understand why anyone had to
choose. I wasn't even sure that people could choose,
although my mother was always saying that if they
really tried, people could be whatever they wanted to
be. But that was just more grown-up talk. As if wanting
to be beautiful (like my mother) could make one bit of
difference in my looks. As if trying to beat up Ian
Forbes could do anything but land me in trouble. As for

being good, I had to admit that I didn't always want to be.

Dear Grandma (I wrote in my next letter): I want to warn you so you won't be disappointed. I'm not always good. Sometimes I don't even try.

It was true. I knew I wasn't supposed to go to the Mud Flats alone, but twice I had managed to sneak off for a quick visit. The boat was gone, already at home on the river, I supposed, but my little friend was there. Each time he had run up to greet me and I had given him an orange. Each time he had called me "American friend" and had walked me back to the Bund.

Of course I knew I was wrong to disobey my mother but that hadn't stopped me. Still, I did feel guilty. If my name had been Marjorie, I thought, I would not have been the sort of person to feel guilty. And if it had not been the end of November, with Christmas already in the air, I might not have thought of the perfect way to solve my problem.

"I know what you can give me for Christmas," I told my mother.

"I've already bought your presents." My mother was writing letters at her little black lacquer desk and she didn't look up.

"This wouldn't cost a thing," I explained. "It would be easy."

"Well?" She still didn't look up.

"You could give me a new name. That's what I really want."

Now she did look up. She even put down her pen. "And what, may I ask, is the matter with the name you have?"

"I don't like it. Take it back." I put my arm around her neck because I didn't want her to feel bad about the mistake she'd made. "Give me the name Marjorie. Just write it on a gift card and put it in a box. You see how easy it would be."

My mother shook her head as if she couldn't understand how I'd got into the family. "I wouldn't name a cat Marjorie," she said.

Well, of course not! "Marjorie is not a cat's name," I yelled. And I stamped out of the room.

When I asked my father, he simply changed the subject. "I know one present you are getting for Christmas," he said, "that you've never even thought of."

He was a good subject-changer.

"Animal, vegetable, or mineral?" I asked.

"Vegetable."

"How heavy?"

"As heavy as a pound of butter." He'd give me no more clues, but of course I did give it a lot of thought between then and Christmas.

But I hadn't forgotten about Marjorie. I was going to Andrea's for the weekend and I would see what she thought.

I loved going to the Hulls'. Not only did they have low ceilings and three children (Andrea, Edward, and David, the adopted one), but the Hull family was different from any I had ever known. They must have believed in goodness because, like us, they were a Y.M.C.A. family, but what they stressed was being free and natural. When the family was alone, for instance, they thought nothing of walking around upstairs without any clothes on. The way Andrea spoke, it was as if she hardly noticed if her parents were naked or not. Moreover, the Hulls seemed to talk together about anything, not as if conversation were divided into Adult subjects and You're-Not-Old-Enough-to-Understand subjects. They discussed whether Adam and Eve had been real people or whether there would ever be another world war. Things like that. And Andrea not only knew how babies were born, she knew exactly how she, herself, had been born.

Since Mr. and Mrs. Hull were in such agreement, you would have thought they would have been happy, but they weren't. According to Andrea, her parents did not get along. She was even afraid they might get a divorce. I had never known anyone who'd had a divorce and I had no way of knowing how married people got along, so of course I was interested in hearing the ups and downs of Mr. and Mrs. Hull's married life. Indeed, I never came back from Andrea's without something new to think about.

My mother was going to take me to the Hulls' on Friday and since my father had a committee meeting that night, she would stay for supper and Mr. Hull would drive her home in his Dodge sedan. I would go home when the Hulls came into town for church on Sunday.

So on Friday I put on my middy blouse which, more than any of my clothes, made me feel like a Marjorie, and my mother called for rickshas. The coolies came running, jostling and swearing at each other, each one shouting for us to take *his* ricksha, take *his*, take *his*. I always felt sorry for the coolies who weren't chosen. I knew how few coppers they made and how often they had to go without rice but, on the other hand, I felt sorry for those who were chosen. The harder a coolie ran and the heavier his load, the sooner he would die. Most ricksha coolies didn't live to be thirty, my father said. Of course I was not a heavy load, but even so, by the time we reached the Hulls' house, my coolie was wiping the sweat from his face, using the dirty rag that hung at his waist. It was no use telling a coolie to walk, not run. He'd feel he was a weakling if he didn't run; he'd lose face.

The Hulls' house was red brick and American-looking, not American like the pictures of my grandmother's house which had a front porch and honeysuckle vines and a swing, but American like a picture in a magazine. Mr. Hull had designed it himself, with special features for his family. Andrea's room, for instance, had a bar down one wall for her to use when she practiced dancing. We went straight to her room and I sat down in her white wicker rocking chair and waited for the news.

"Well, I'm afraid they are doomed," she sighed. Her parents had had a terrible fight the week before, she reported, and hadn't spoken for days. "And they won't listen to me. I figured out how we could bring our whole family together but they won't listen."

Andrea was lying flat on the floor because that was good for her posture, but with news like this, I was surprised that she still cared about her posture.

"What did you figure out?" I asked.

"A baby." Andrea gave me time to get used to the idea. "I didn't expect my mother to have the baby," she explained. "That would take too long. I wanted my parents to adopt one from the same place that they adopted David. Then we'd all have someone we could love together." She began pedaling her legs in the air to strengthen her thighs. "Besides," she added, "an adopted baby would be good for David. He wouldn't feel so left out. You know how he is."

I did know. At twelve, David was the oldest of the children. The Hulls had adopted him when they

thought they couldn't have children of their own. Then a year later Andrea had come along and afterwards Edward, but Mr. and Mrs. Hull treated David the same as the others and seemed to love him as much. Still, David felt different. He was always wondering who his real mother and father were, even though the Hulls said they didn't know, couldn't find out, and it didn't matter. They didn't even want him to talk about it and he didn't, except sometimes to Andrea and me.

Andrea let her legs drop to the floor and rolled over to look at me. "They weren't even interested in a baby," she said. "But guess what?"

"What?"

"They decided it would be nice to invite an orphan here for Christmas vacation. So they wrote to the orphanage and we heard yesterday. We're going to have a girl. Eleven years old. She'll arrive by boat three days before Christmas and stay through New Year's."

"What's her name?"

"Millie." Andrea screwed up her face. "Ugh."

I agreed that the name was not good. But an orphan! I'd like an orphan sleeping in my house and spending Christmas with me. "Maybe you could call her Lee for short," I suggested.

Later at supper Mrs. Hull told my mother about Millie's coming. As soon as she was finished, I spoke up.

"Why couldn't we . . ." I began, but Mrs. Hull interrupted. She turned to my mother.

"We could share Millie," she said. "She could go to your house for a few days in the middle of her stay. I expect Jean would like that."

That wasn't what I'd had in mind, but still it sounded like a good idea. So it was settled that when the Hulls came to our house for Christmas dinner (which they always did), they would leave Millie with us for three days. (In my mind I was already calling her Lee. She'd be more like a sister, I decided, than a friend.)

I was still thinking about Lee when we went to bed, although I didn't usually bother with private thoughts when I was going to bed at Andrea's. The Hulls believed in fresh air, so they had a sleeping porch where the whole family slept, winter and summer, with the windows wide open around three sides of the room. When I came for a visit, Mr. and Mrs. Hull slept in their own room and I used their bed. Sometimes before going to sleep, David and Andrea and Edward (who was only six) and I played Pioneer. We'd roll the beds into a semicircle and fight off the horse thieves. Sometimes we played War and lined up the beds for the wounded. Maybe because it was later than usual, tonight we didn't play anything. Andrea got under the covers and began right away to shake her head from side to side on the pillow, which was the way she went to sleep. Sometimes she had to shake her head a long time but not tonight. I had decided that I was the only one awake when I saw David sit up.

"Jean?" he whispered. "You awake? I want to ask a favor."

I couldn't imagine what David Hull could want of me. I did understand, however, that it wasn't easy for him to ask. He was a pale, thin-faced, twitchy boy who, I had to admit, seemed out of place in the Hull family with their free and natural ways.

"I want it to be a secret." His whisper had turned hoarse.

I got up, pulled a blanket off my bed, wrapped myself up, and went to sit on his bed.

"You know that Millie," he said.

"Yes."

"Well, she comes from the same orphans' home as I came from. And I was thinking. They must have records in the office of that place." He was looking out the window and shivering as he talked.

"Why couldn't she sneak into that office when she goes back after being here? Why couldn't she find out about me?" He took such a big breath I could feel the favor coming.

"Then she could write you. And you could tell me. That way, Mom and Dad wouldn't have to know anything about it. You know how they are."

The whole idea sounded crazy. "David," I said, "why do you care so much? What difference does it make?"

He turned on me, his face fiercer than I'd known it could be. "How would you like it," he hissed, "if you didn't know whether your father was a crook or what he was? Or whether he was dead or alive? If you didn't know that you were American? You might be Russian or Danish or German or anything. How would you like it?"

Well, of course, I knew I wouldn't like it. "But you're legally an American," I pointed out.

"Legally! What difference does that make?" David's whisper was becoming raspier and raspier. "When you go back to America, you'll know you're home. When you meet your grandmother, you'll know she's your real grandmother. I won't know anything." He spoke so fast it was as if he'd learned his thoughts by heart. "You see?" he asked.

"Yes."

"Well, will you or won't you? Will you make the plans with Millie?"

"Yes," I said, "I will." But as I went back to bed, my

feelings were tangled up again. Part of me said that I had to help him; part of me said I couldn't help him. In the first place, the idea wouldn't work; in the second place, David would never be satisfied. No matter what he found out, he would always want to know more.

From across the room came his whisper, quieter now. "Thanks," he said. "But remember. Don't even tell Andrea."

As it turned out, Andrea and I were so busy the next day, I wasn't even tempted to tell. As soon as we got up, she announced that we were going to wash our hair. She had a new rinse made from dried camomile flowers. "It brings out the hidden lights in your hair," she explained. Andrea had different shades of gold already in her hair, but I didn't see what could be hidden in my plain brown hair. Certainly I never dreamed I could have undiscovered red highlights but Andrea said I could; I just needed to encourage them to come out. And of course I was willing to do that. So Andrea dropped the dried, buttonlike flowers in a pitcher of hot water, and while they soaked, we began washing our hair, each of us soaping each other and giving each other a first rinse with ordinary water.

Then for the magic rinse. I poured half the pitcher of camomile mixture over Andrea's head and she poured the other half over mine. I rushed to the mirror.

"Wait until it dries," Andrea said.

So I rubbed my head with a towel, stopping every few minutes for a look. No sign of red yet. I kept rubbing until at last Andrea (whose hair was a-glint) told me to quit. As soon as I'd combed my hair, she inspected it and assured me that there was a change. "Wait until the sun shines on it," she said. "That's when it really shows up." I smiled as I fluffed out my hair. I had never appreciated its possibilities before.

After breakfast we walked on top of the wall that separated the Hulls' property from the Chinese farms. It was an eight-foot-high wall and when you stood on it, you felt as if you owned the world. Today with the air crisp and the sun making highlights on my hair, I felt especially pleased with that world. It was like a picture postcard. Across the background a water buffalo walked with a boy on its back. The rest of the picture was divided neatly into little farm plots, each with its mud hut, each with its creaking well. From this height the people didn't look like poor, overworked Chinese; they seemed to be toy people going happily about their business. And I felt like a queen, walking the turret of my castle. I waved my arm at the scene below.

"That's our kingdom," I announced to Andrea. "And I am Queen Marjorie. Who are you?"

"You are Queen—who?"

"Marjorie."

Andrea gave me the same kind of withering look as my mother had. "Marjorie is not a name for a queen," she said. "It's not a decent name for anyone."

I felt myself getting mad, so to be safe, I sat down, my feet dangling over the Chinese side of the wall.

"I happen to like the name Marjorie," I said stiffly. "I guess I can be Queen-anything-I-want-to-be. What's your name?"

Andrea was sitting down too. "Queen Zobeide."

I didn't have the chance to tell her what I thought of her name. Actually both of us forgot all about being queens because at that moment an old woman stepped out of a hut and started shrieking and cursing at a man in the next farmyard. She shook her fists. "Egg of a turtle!" she screamed. "May all your children fall sick! May you outlive every one of them! May the gods heap misfortune on your head!" On and on.

At night lying on the sleeping porch, Andrea and I had often heard women carrying on like this. Now we were trying so hard to catch all the language, not to miss a word, that we were surprised when at the height of her rage the woman stopped short. There was a moment of complete silence. The woman had caught sight of us, sitting on our wall, staring. She put her hands on her hips, threw back her head, and called on all the gods and neighbors to come and witness the dog-things in their midst. It was as if now, *now* she had at last found someone worthy of her anger. She could forget the poor pig of a man who lived next door. For us she found new words so bad we couldn't translate them, although our Chinese was as good as our English. As her voice grew more shrill, her neighbors did come to listen and look. Occasionally a man would laugh and add an insult. Young boys began picking up stones and hurling them at the wall. "Foreign devils," they shouted. "Foreign devils."

Andrea and I were used to being called "foreign devil." We were used to insults. Coolies often spat directly in our path, but we had been taught to act as if we didn't see, as if nothing had happened. But today it was different. More people angry all together, angrier than before. We knew the stones wouldn't reach us; still, we couldn't get down from that wall fast enough.

As soon as we were off the ladder, we slid to the ground, out of breath. "I guess it will get worse," Andrea said. "It's the Communists who are doing this. They're the ones who are making the Chinese so mad."

Of course I knew about the Communists who wanted to make a revolution in China like the one in Russia that had driven Vera Sebastian out. Still, I hadn't paid much attention. All my life there had been fighting somewhere in China—warlord against warlord. Grown-ups were constantly talking about these warlords, hoping that one of them would finally bring the country together in peace. When a warlord was a Christian (and one or two were), my father really got his hopes up. But I just thought of the Communists as another group of Chinese. Fighting as always.

But it wasn't like that, Andrea said. If the Communists got the chance, there would be a new kind of war. Farmers against their landlords. Factory workers against factory owners. The poor against the rich. Chinese against foreigners. "The Communists want to get us out," she said. "My father says that one day we may be glad to have those gunboats in the river to protect us."

It all sounded so complicated, I thought of my father when he was discouraged. Sometimes he'd put out his hands in a kind of helpless gesture. "But China's so big," he'd say, as if he were apologizing for having come so far and doing so little. That's the way I felt now. China was too big for me to even imagine all the things that might happen. At the moment all I hoped was that the Communists wouldn't spoil Christmas.

But after the weekend when I got home, I was glad to see that Christmas seemed to be coming on in the usual way. We had mailed our packages to America months ago. (I had sent my grandmother a doily filled with nothing but French knots. It was a "labor of love," I explained.) Now big, bulky packages were arriving from America, pasted over with seals that said, DO NOT OPEN UNTIL DECEMBER 25. Of course I knew what my grandmother had sent me because every year she sent the same thing. I didn't blame her. Without having met me, how could she know that I hated to get clothes for Christmas? Besides, she had made every one of the petticoats she sent, so they were probably labors of love too.

In addition to the American packages, presents were being delivered to my parents from Chinese friends. Almost every day when I came home from school I'd find one or two cakes on the hall table, waiting to be put away. They were all alike—tall, castlelike cakes, each with white icing and pink characters that said LONG LIFE AND HAPPINESS and sprinkled all over with tiny silver pellets that my mother wouldn't let me eat.

I was also buying presents to give away. For Lee I had bought a red pencil box with two drawers in it, like mine. A package of open-up paper flowers. And I had gone into the sandalwood box where I kept my savings and taken out twenty coppers and four twenty-cent pieces. I had them changed into a silver dollar and put it in a velvet-lined jewelry case my mother had. Although it was hard to take so much money out of my savings all at once, I figured that orphans would hardly ever have money of their own, certainly not as much as a whole dollar. My mother, who was positive that Lee would like clothes, was knitting a sweater and a pair of mittens.

I had thought so much about Lee that by Christmas Eve I felt I knew her. I pictured how much more comfortable she'd be with me than with a sleeping porch full of children and with grown-ups who might or might not be speaking to each other. I wished she could have been with us to help decorate the tree and hang the red crepe paper streamers in the dining room, but I knew I shouldn't expect life to be one-hundred-percent perfect. It was enough that she was coming the next day. And if we really became good friends—well, who knew what might happen? After all, orphans could be adopted.

I bargained with my parents about what time we'd get up in the morning. "Six o'clock," I suggested. "Seven," my father countered. "Six-thirty," I offered. He accepted. He even agreed not to shave until after we had opened our presents. Our guests wouldn't be arriving until one o'clock. Eleven guests altogether: the Hulls, Lee, two elderly missionary ladies who would otherwise be alone at Christmas, and three sailors (whom we'd never met) from an American gunboat.

What I liked best about Christmas was that for a whole day grown-ups seemed to agree to take time off from being grown-ups. At six-thirty sharp when I burst into my parents' room, yelling "Merry Christmas!," they both laughed and jumped right up as if six-thirty wasn't an early hour at all. By the time we came downstairs, the servants were lined up in the hall dressed in their best. "Gung-shi." They bowed. "Gung-shi. Gung-shi." This was the way Chinese offered congratulations on special occasions, and the greeting, as it was repeated, sounded like little bells tinkling. Lin Nai-Nai, however, didn't "gung-shi." For months she had been waiting for this day. She stepped forward. "Merry Christmas," she said just as if she could have said anything in English that she wanted to. I was so proud, I took her hand as we all trooped into the living room. My father lighted the tree and he distributed the first gifts of the day—red envelopes filled with money for the servants. After a flurry of more "gung-shis," the servants left and there were the three of us in front of a huge mound of packages. All mysteries.

I kept telling myself that we wanted to make Christmas last but whenever it was my turn to open a package, I yanked at the ribbons and tore off the paper because I couldn't wait. When I had finished, I was sitting inside a circle of presents: four books, a fountain pen, an Uncle Wiggily game, a stamp album, a skipping rope, a pocketbook, a bracelet, a paperweight with snow falling inside, and best of all, the "pound of butter" present—a box of pale blue stationery with my name JEAN GUTTERY and HANKOW, CHINA printed in gold at the top with a little gold pagoda at each side. And of course there were clothes, including the petticoat from my grandmother, one size larger than last year's. But I felt strange when I thought of my grandmother. Here I was in the middle of Christmas and there she was with Christmas not even started in her house. It was only December 24 in America.

I was watching out the window when the Hulls arrived. As soon as the Dodge sedan drew up, a back door flew open and Andrea jumped out. By the time she reached the door, I was there.

"Call her Millie," she whispered. "She hates Lee."

David was behind. "She's shy," he said, whispering too. "And hard to talk to. But remember, you promised."

Edward followed, pushing past to get to the Christmas tree.

Back at the car Mrs. Hull was standing at one side, bending over and looking in. Even from the back she looked like someone who studied American fashion magazines. Mr. Hull was standing on the other side of the car, also bending over. They were obviously talking to Millie. After a few minutes Mr. Hull straightened up and came to the house, carrying Millie's suitcase. Mrs. Hull and Millie followed.

I was surprised at Millie. I guess I expected everyone to look happy on Christmas, but I could tell by the way she walked with her head down that she wasn't happy. When she reached the door and did look up, what struck me was her expression. She had the same secretive, stubborn look that Vera Sebastian had. Well, she was scared, I told myself. I would be scared too if I were in her place.

I grinned in a way that was supposed to show that at least I wasn't anyone to be scared of. "Come on up and see my room," I said.

She followed.

"Bring your suitcase," I suggested.

Her suitcase was standing inside the front door but she didn't turn around. "No," she said. "Not now."

Upstairs I showed her not only my room but all the rooms and each time she said, "Uh-huh." By the end of the tour I was talking so loud, it was as if I thought she was deaf. "Let's go downstairs," I said. "Your presents are under the tree."

Sitting beside the tree, Millie opened her packages slowly, careful to untie the ribbons, careful not to tear the paper. Each time she said "Thank you" dutifully as if she'd been told to say it. She did seem to like her sweater because she put it on, and I noticed that when she thought no one was looking, she took the silver dollar out of its box and slipped it into her sweater pocket. When she had finally finished, Andrea and I tore open our gifts to each other. A can of camomile flowers for me, a package of fortune-telling cards for her.

The other guests arrived now and at my mother's nod, I made the rounds, dropping a British School curtsy to each one. I only did it to please my mother, but it was a mistake. The missionary ladies tried to be cute and, giggling, they curtsied back. Andrea looked ready to throw up and the sailors, who had obviously not been in a curtsying crowd before, blushed. Fortunately Wong Sze-Fu, the serving boy, saved the day by announcing that dinner was ready, so we trooped into the dining room. The turkey, surrounded by a ring of candied red apples, sat on a silver platter at my father's place. Rising triumphantly from the center of the table was a butter pagoda, unusually tall and splendid. As we sat down, I thought that now things would be better. Once we started eating, people would perk up and be jolly. Maybe even Millie.

What I hadn't counted on was that those three sailors would be quite so shy. I could see that they wanted to be friendly but didn't know how. So my father began talking about Christmas at home in Pennsylvania and before long all the grown-ups were talking about old Christmases. The sailors told about their families in New Jersey and Illinois and Ohio and the missionary ladies chimed in about Michigan and Maryland and Mr. Hull described Christmas in Los Angeles, California, and Mrs. Hull said, no, it wasn't like that at all. Of course this left the children with nothing to talk about. Not one of us had been to a single state in America.

Well, I thought, after dinner we'd go into the living room and sing around the piano. Then things would be better. But when the time came, Millie didn't want to sing. She sat on the couch, and although Andrea and I urged her, she wouldn't even join in for "Deck the Halls," my favorite. She wouldn't come to the piano when Phillip, the sailor from New Jersey, asked her, even though he was the cutest of the three sailors and I didn't see how anyone could turn him down.

Andrea looked at me and shrugged as if she'd given

up, but when the missionary ladies and the sailors left, Millie suddenly seemed to come to life. Edward suggested that we children should play hide-and-seek, and right away Millie smiled as if she'd been waiting for something like this. "Let's," she said.

David said he'd be "it," and as the five of us ran into the hall to start the game, I took Millie's hand.

"You can hide with me," I said.

"Thanks, but I'd rather hide by myself." Millie answered in a tone that was almost friendly, so I didn't feel bad. And since I'd shown her the house, I didn't suppose she'd get lost.

While everyone scattered, I crept into my favorite hiding place, the little closet tucked under the stairs. I closed the door and although I could just barely hear David beginning to count, in a few minutes I couldn't even hear that. Scrunched up on the floor in the dark, I planned how Millie and I would play Uncle Wiggily after everyone had left. I suppose the time passed faster than I thought, for suddenly I realized that it had been quite a while since I'd heard anything. Surely I would have heard pounding steps or at least one "Home free!" but when I opened the door and crawled out, I couldn't see any signs of the game.

My mother and father were standing in the hall, looking unhappy.

"Where's everybody?" I asked. Then I noticed that Millie's suitcase that had been standing by the front door was gone.

"Where's Millie?" I shouted.

The way my mother and father led me into the living room, I knew that everything had gone wrong. Everything. My mother explained: As soon as the game had started, Millie had taken her suitcase and run out to the

Hulls' car. The grown-ups had heard the front door closing, so they had investigated.

"No one could do anything with her," my mother said. "So they went home."

"How could they?" I was crying. "How could they sneak off like that without even saying good-bye to me?"

"Oh, Jean," my mother sighed, "it happened so quickly. David was trying to pull Millie out of the car and Mrs. Hull was getting mad at Mr. Hull and right in the middle of everything Mr. Hull told everyone to get in the car and he just drove off." She put her arms around me. "I know," she said. "I know."

"Even if Millie had stayed," my father said, "you wouldn't have had a good time."

"She didn't like me," I sniffled.

"She didn't seem to like anyone." My father pulled his handkerchief out of his breast pocket so I could blow my nose. It was then I noticed that Millie's pencil box and paper flowers and Andrea's fortune-telling cards were still under the tree and I began to feel sorry for myself all over again. Oh, I knew the Hulls would feel bad—especially David—but I didn't have room for anyone's feelings but my own. I picked up my snowflake paperweight and I shook it and shook it. I shook until the snow came down in a perfect fury of a storm.

"After supper we'll go upstairs, you and I, and start reading one of your new books together," my mother suggested. "How would you like that?"

"All right."

Usually I loved it when my mother lay down on my bed and we got interested in a new story together, but somehow tonight when my mother kicked off her shoes and stretched out beside me, I didn't want a book. She was still dressed in her black velvet dress and her pearls. She still smelled of lavender sachet and I just wanted her to talk.

"Tell me about when you were a little girl in Washington, P.A.," I said. (My parents always called their hometown in Pennsylvania, Washington, P.A.)

So my mother told me the old stories about her pet cat, Kitty Gray, who had been so mean and about her sister Blanche's pet cat, Big Puss, who had been so sweet. She told how her brother George used to chase her and Blanche out of his tree house and how rough their older sister, Sarah, had been when she gave them their baths.

"And what did you do when she rubbed too hard?" I asked.

My mother laughed. "Why, we splashed her. Yes, until she was wet right through her apron."

"You and Aunt Blanche don't sound as if you were always good."

My mother was still smiling. "I guess we weren't."

"Then how come," I asked, "that you expect me to be one-hundred-percent perfect?"

My mother snapped back from her little-girl time. "All I want you to do is try," she said.

I wished I had never asked. I wished she had never answered. But what I said next came as a surprise even to me. I propped myself up on my elbow.

"Why can't we adopt a baby?" I asked. "Not an eleven-year-old. A baby. Why not?"

Sometimes when my mother was given a hard question, she'd say, "Maybe" or "We'll see." Not tonight.

"Well, we can't," she said. Then quickly she began talking about Washington, P.A., again.

And I began thinking about my grandmother. I wondered if she would put my doily on her dining-room table. After my mother had said "good night" and left the room, I got up and went to my desk. I took out the first sheet of my brand-new stationery.

Dear Grandma, (I wrote): Thank you so much for the petticoat. It is lovely.

I didn't want to spoil my stationery by writing the whole truth about our Christmas, so I just told her what I got and signed my name, along with love and kisses.

Then I added a P.S. on the back.

How do you like the name Marjorie? (I wrote).

I still thought that if my name were Marjorie, things might be different.

3

ONCE THE REVOLUTION BEGAN IN EARNEST IN Hankow, it was impossible to ignore it. Every few days there was a strike of some sort. Student strikes. Worker strikes. Coolie strikes. There were demonstrations and marches and agitators haranguing about how foreigners ought to be kicked out of China and how poor people should take money from the rich. Even our servants listened to the agitators. Once Lin Nai-Nai came home and told my mother that a wonderful thing was going to happen in China. All the money in the country would be gathered up and divided equally so that there would no longer be rich people and poor people.

"If they do that," my mother said, "maybe you won't have as much money as you do now. There are many more poor people in China than there are rich."

But I could tell that Lin Nai-Nai thought that the money dividing would be part of a great new China where men would stick to one wife and women wouldn't bind their feet.

Once an agitator gathered a crowd around him in front of the Y.M.C.A. building. He shouted about the Y.M.C.A. being a foreign organization with a foreigner in charge who should be run out of town. The man in charge, of course, was my father and when he heard what was going on, he slipped quietly out the front door of the building so that he was standing behind the agitator without the agitator seeing him. My father put his hands casually in his pockets and cocked his head as he listened to the man carrying on. Then my father smiled and winked at the crowd as if it were a huge joke that the agitator should be calling my father names while my father was right there behind him. The crowd thought it was a joke too and laughed. Of course the agitator lost face and that was the end of that. My father was lucky, but at the same time he had many Chinese friends, even among the coolies. Some of his friends were for the Communists, some were against, but my father had made up his mind not to take sides. He worked in the Y.M.C.A. so he could help those Chinese who needed help in whatever way they needed it.

Occasionally there were riots. The first time the riot siren blew, we were eating supper. My father, who was a member of the riot squad (organized to help put down riots, with tear bombs if necessary), rushed out of the house and my mother began pacing. She hadn't been feeling well lately and I could tell that she certainly didn't feel well now. She had me sleep in a cot in her room that night, and after I got into bed, she sat down beside me.

"I want to tell you something, Jean," she said. "No matter what I ask you to do tonight, I want you just to do it. No questions. No arguments."

It was on the tip of my tongue to ask, "Like what?" but I realized that was a question in itself. Of course I knew what my mother was afraid of. She thought a mob might burst into the house and she wanted to hide me, but I wasn't sure that she knew the best places or would even think of the closet under the stairs. And I wasn't sure that she was planning to hide with me. Still, I didn't say anything.

She lay down on her bed with her clothes on, but I knew her eyes were open, just as mine were. We were both listening, but all we heard were the usual night sounds. A beggar woman crying for money to bury her dead baby. Dogs howling. Every night ten greyhounds that belonged to the Frenchman across the street wailed as if the world were coming to an end.

But we heard no fighting. I spent the time deciding how I would save my mother instead of letting her save me, but as it turned out, neither of us had to do any saving. About three o'clock in the morning Mr. Hull came into the yard below our window and called to my mother.

Both of us ran out on the balcony.

"Arthur's all right," he said. "It's all over. Everything's under control. He'll be back in about an hour." He talked some more but I didn't listen. I just stood on the balcony, looking up at the night sky, at the crook of the moon, at the spangle of stars—each one in its proper place.

Oh, Grandma, I thought, that is the same moon and the same stars that will be over your grape arbor and your henhouse tomorrow. It was almost too hard to believe.

There was upheaval all around me that spring, and although it was often scary, it was also hazy, like passages in a book that you just skim over. "We're living right in the middle of history," my father would say, but it seemed to me I could understand long-ago history better than history today. All I hoped was that however this revolution turned out, Lin Nai-Nai would get her wishes. And I hoped that all the people who had drawn rotten lives would be given a change of luck.

As for me, I went on with my own life—going to school, learning poetry, reading. Twice I managed to take an orange to my little friend in the Mud Flats. Actually the worst thing that happened to me had nothing to do with the revolution. My father came home one evening with the news that Mr. Hull had been transferred to the Shanghai Y.M.C.A. The whole family would move the next week. I felt as if I'd had the wind knocked out of me and I knew that I wouldn't have time to get it back before they'd be gone.

They came for dinner the night before they left. I hadn't even tried to imagine how the Hulls would feel about the move, but since I felt bad, I took for granted that they would too. But they were excited, all except David. Ever since Christmas, David had stopped getting excited about anything. Sometimes I felt like shaking him and telling him to quit feeling so sorry for himself, but tonight I didn't care how David Hull felt.

As soon as we were alone, Andrea began talking about Shanghai. They were going to live in a house with five modern bathrooms, she said. She was going to take dancing lessons from an Austrian dancer named Hans. And she'd go to the Shanghai American School.

"Shanghai is so much more up-to-date than Hankow," she said. "More like the States."

"Since when have you been calling America 'the States'?" I asked.

Andrea just tossed her head as if that were too silly a question to answer.

"My mother is going to have her hair bobbed when we get there," she said. "And my father says that's all right with him. Ever since we heard about Shanghai, they've been nice to each other."

I could understand why Andrea was excited. I'd be excited just to have the five modern bathrooms, but right then I couldn't think of a single thing to be happy about.

"Well, you've got something to look forward to too," Andrea said.

I couldn't imagine what.

"It won't be long now," she said.

I supposed she must mean summer vacation. It was true. I certainly did look forward to the three months we spent every summer in Peitaiho on the ocean north of Peking. Once we had gone to the mountains in Kuling which was nearer and beautiful too. But not like Peitaiho. The most glorious moment of the whole year was when I first caught sight of the ocean. We'd be riding donkeys from the train station to our house on the beach when, halfway up a hill, the ocean would suddenly come into view. The blueness of it rolling on and on right out to the sky made something inside me leap. Free, I thought. The ocean made me feel free. Free of school and grown-ups, free of goodness and badness and ugliness and loneliness. Sometimes in the winter when I walked past the beggars in Hankow, I would think of Peitaiho and be glad to know that it was in the same world.

"Yes," I told Andrea, "I do look forward to Peitaiho."

"How's your mother feeling?"

I shrugged. It wasn't as if my mother were sick enough to stay in bed. I thought Andrea gave me a funny look but right away she put her hand on my arm.

"We'll write," she said. "Probably sometime you'll visit us and then you can have a bathroom all to yourself."

As soon as Andrea had left town, I began concentrating on Peitaiho. I made pictures in my mind of the summer until the pictures became so real I could leaf through them like pages in an album. A picture of us having a picnic on the Great Wall. (We did this once each summer.) Pictures of my father and me wading at low tide from rock to rock, chipping off oysters for our supper. A picture of us sitting on the porch at sunset, watching the sky flame up and then drift off into pinks and purples. "That's the best one yet," we'd say.

My mother and father were both so busy these days I could never find time for us to go through my pictures together. But one Sunday morning when my father was shaving, I decided that I couldn't keep the summer to myself any longer. I often watched my father shave on Sunday when he was in no hurry. He'd stand in front of the mirror in his trousers, his suspenders loose over his undershirt, and he'd lather up his face until the lather stood in peaks like whipped cream. Since we didn't have a modern bathroom, he'd shave over an enamel basin and use hot water from a pitcher. (The bathtub, round like a big green salad bowl, took so many pitchers of water you never sat in more than a puddle.)

I leaned against the doorframe while my father twisted his face to shave down one side.

"How do you suppose the oysters will be this summer?" I asked. "Do you think this will be the year I'll find a pearl?" (I always hoped.)

My father put down his razor and straightened his face. "I've been meaning to tell you," he said. "We can't go to Peitaiho this summer, Jean. We'll be going to Kuling."

I couldn't believe it. There he was with soap over one half of his face, saying Kuling, not Peitaiho, just as if he were saying cornflakes, not Grape-Nuts.

"What do you mean—*can't*?"

"With all the trouble in Hankow," he said, "I can't be so far away. I'll have to travel back and forth."

"Well, why don't you tell me things?" I shouted.

"Why couldn't I have been around while you were still deciding? You think it's easy for me to throw away all my plans just like that?"

"We just decided last week," my father said.

"Then we'll never go to Peitaiho again," I pointed out. We'd be leaving China in April of the next year and we'd be in America the next summer. "Never." I hated the word *never* and hoped that, hearing it, my father might find some way to change our plans.

"Maybe we should put off going to America."

"You know I don't mean that." My father had no business trying to turn this into a joke.

He sighed as he picked up his razor, but the soap on his face had dried and he had to wipe it off and begin again. "I know you're disappointed," he said. "And I'm sorry. But you'll like Kuling. You've just forgotten it."

"I haven't forgotten how you go up the mountain."

"You're older now; you won't be scared."

"Mother is a grown-up," I reminded him, "and she was scared." Who wouldn't be? The only way up the mountain to Kuling was by sedan chair. Two coolies, one in front and one in back (four or even six coolies if the person were heavy), carried the shafts of your chair up a narrow, pebbly, dirt path that twisted its way up the steep mountain. Sometimes going around a sharp corner, your chair would swing right over the edge of the mountain. If a coolie stumbled, there was no place for a person in a chair to go but over and down.

Of course I understood why we had to go to Kuling, but that didn't make me feel any less cross. Since it was Sunday, I felt cross anyway because, as far as I was concerned, Sunday was a lost day. Not only did I have to sit through Sunday School and church, but even after that I couldn't be natural. I wasn't allowed to embroider on Sunday, for instance. Or skip rope. Or play games. The only thing that I liked about the day was singing hymns. When I came to a line like "Fight manfully onward," I could believe that if I held out, one day I might really get to Washington, P.A.

But this Sunday in church we sang no "onward" hymns and needless to say, I didn't listen to Dr. Carhart's sermon. Instead I played my usual climbing game. There were more rafters in that Union Church than I've ever seen in any building. The whole ceiling was a maze of rafters crisscrossing and flying up from wooden columns on the floor. In my mind I would shinny up one of those columns and then work my way from rafter to rafter, figuring out how to make my next move, seeing how far I could get.

Today I was balancing myself just above the altar when I heard Dr. Carhart say that he knew what death was like. I hung tight to the rafter. Of course I wondered about death since grown-ups never talked about it, at least in front of me. Sometimes waking up in the middle of the night, I would think right away about death, as if the idea were just waiting in the dark to pop out of me. Well, Dr. Carhart said that he'd once taken a train from Switzerland to Italy and at the border the train went through a long dark tunnel. Then suddenly it burst out of the tunnel into a blaze of light and you were in Italy. That's what death was like, he said. It was a glory. Nothing to feel sad about.

I had to admit he made it sound interesting. Maybe everyone should travel from Switzerland to Italy, I thought, just for practice. Yet why couldn't I believe Dr. Carhart? He was a grown-up and a preacher; he ought to know what he was talking about. But part of me was never sure about grown-ups.

Personally, I was certain I'd prefer Peitaiho to Italy. Indeed, I never stopped being sorry that we weren't going there, but I did feel better one day in the middle of May when my father said we were going to Kuling early. Before school was over.

On the day before we left, I took a note from my mother to Miss Williams, explaining my absence for the rest of the term.

"But you'll miss your examinations," Miss Williams said after she'd read the note.

"Yes, Miss Williams," I smiled.

"I don't know how I can give you a report card."

I kept smiling.

"You know you have done very poorly in arithmetic."

"Yes, Miss Williams."

"Well, perhaps you'll just have to take the examinations in September and get your report then."

Somehow I couldn't stop smiling. September? Why should I worry about September now?

The next morning when we got on the boat for the trip to Kiukiang where we'd start up the mountain, I thought: Ta-ta, Miss Williams. Ta-ta, Ian Forbes and Vera Sebastian and the king of England. I was off and away! Two whole days and one night on the Yangtse.

Why did I love the river so? It wasn't what you would call beautiful. It wasn't *like* anything. It just *was* and it had always been. When you were on the river or even looking at it, you flowed with time. You were part of forever. At first I looked among all the boats we passed for a new junk that might be mine, but after a while I decided it didn't matter. My boat was somewhere out there. Wide-awake, eyes peeled.

I was so happy on the river that I had put the mountain trip out of my mind until we were actually in Kiu-kiang and I could see the mountains rearing up in the background. We had made friends on the boat with two young Catholic priests from New Jersey who were also going to Kuling, so we included them in our party. After spending a night in a hotel in Kiukiang, we went by car across the plains (rice fields on either side of us) to the base of the mountain where we rented our sedan chairs.

It was a hot day. We all wore pith helmets to protect us from the sun except Lin Nai-Nai who wore a Chinese straw hat. One of the priests led our procession; my mother came next, then my father, me, the other priest, and Lin Nai-Nai. Behind us came a string of coolies with our luggage strapped on their backs.

I had decided that I would not look to my right over the edge of the mountain at any time. Still, I could tell when the mountain became steep. My chair tilted back; the coolies stopped talking and began grunting. The muscles bulged in the legs of my father's coolies and the sweat poured down their bodies. I knew we were really high when the priest behind me called out to the priest in the front of the line.

"Just look at that, will you?" he yelled. "That must be three thousand feet straight down."

I closed my eyes. Why didn't that priest just shut up and pray? I wondered. But no, he went right on. "What a view! You never saw anything like that in Paterson, did you?"

Pray, I begged him silently as I gripped the arms of my chair.

My coolies slowed down, shifting the shafts of my chair, feeling for their footing, so I knew we were going around a corner. I must be out over the edge.

Oh, God, I prayed, just get me out of here safely and I'll never ask another favor of you.

A few moments later the priest must have been over the edge. And what did he say? "Wow!" That's all. Just—wow. I was surprised he hadn't flunked religion.

I didn't know that we had actually reached Kuling until I felt my chair being thumped down on the ground and I heard the welcoming voices of Mr. and Mrs. Jordan, whose house we'd be sharing. A Y.M.C.A. couple from another city, the Jordans had often visited us in Hankow and I knew I liked them.

I was stiff when I got out of my chair, so while my father was paying the coolies and we were saying goodbye to the priests and hello to the Jordans, I walked about. My mother came and put her arm around my shoulders. She seemed tired and pale after the ride up the mountain, but now that we were here, we both looked at the scenery for the first time. At the violet and blue mountains. At the pink and red azaleas that were scattered with such abandon over the hillsides.

"Isn't the color wonderful?" my mother whispered. She sounded as if she were afraid to raise her voice for fear the color would fade into Hankow gray.

"Yes." I couldn't get enough of looking. My eyes must have been starved for color and I hadn't known it.

"And do you hear that?"

What I heard sounded like a stream and tumbling water.

"That's Rattling Brook," my mother said. "We'll explore tomorrow."

Right now we went into the house and let Mrs. Jordan show us around. The front porch was for warm days and sunsets, she said, and the glassed-in porch was for rainy times. Mrs. Jordan turned to me. "But I think what you are going to like best," she said, "is your room."

Upstairs she opened the door to a room in the back of the house. The first thing I noticed was that the windows faced the mountains so I'd always be looking up and not down. And there was a window seat. And a little desk painted blue with shiny black knobs on the drawers. And a bookcase with books in it.

"Whoever had this room before was crazy about the Bobbsey Twins," Mrs. Jordan said. "I think that's the whole set there. They may be too young for you but you'll find some old copies of *St. Nicholas* magazine."

At each new discovery, I said "Oh" as if that were the only word for joy that had been invented, but when I looked at my bed, I said, "Ohhh." Right in the middle of the bed, curled up like a cushion, was a tiger cat with a white bib. I sank down on my knees beside the bed and put my hand gently on the cat's fur. She opened her eyes and blinked at me as if she'd just been waiting for me to come along.

"Is she yours?" I asked Mrs. Jordan.

I saw Mrs. Jordan and my mother smile at each other. "She's yours," Mrs. Jordan said. "She just walked in last week and made herself at home." Mrs. Jordan explained that when she'd first come, they'd called her *Ke-ren,* the Chinese word for "guest," but when she made it clear that she was staying, they shortened it to Kurry.

I liked everything about my room so much that I hardly felt I needed an outside to my world, but the next morning when my mother and I went exploring, I could see that the outside was far better than the inside.

First, we went behind the house and between two banks of azaleas we found Rattling Brook, gurgling and bouncing topsy-turvy over stones.

"May I put my feet in?"

My mother nodded. The brook was obviously too stony for wading, so when I'd taken off my shoes and socks, I sat on the bank and let the water dance over my bare toes and splash up my legs.

Later we walked up the hill, looking for wild flowers. Actually, we didn't need to look. They were everywhere—buttercups, daisies, wild roses, violets. When my mother came across an unusual one, she would give an "Oh" of joy and tell me its name: daphne, wild heliotrope, pink orchid. Sometimes we'd stop and look up at the mountains and at the scarves of fog they wore around their shoulders. There were eagles up there people said and mountain lions maybe. My mother sat down on the ground and threw her head back to look at the sky. She was wearing her new blue dress, one of the loose dresses she'd made to keep her cool, and I thought I'd never seen her look so pretty. I thought I've never loved her quite so much.

That night I went to sleep listening to Rattling Brook and when I came down to breakfast the next morning, Mrs. Jordan told me that my mother was in the hospital. She had gone in the middle of the night and my father was still there with her. I pushed my plate of fried eggs away from me. "What's wrong?" I asked.

"She had pain in her legs," Mrs. Jordan said.

Later when I asked Lin Nai-Nai what was wrong, she pointed to her middle and shook her head. So there was something wrong with her middle too. I didn't want to think about it. I looked over the Bobbsey Twin books and decided that it didn't matter which one I started since the Bobbsey Twins had been everywhere and done everything. I took the one that told about them on the seashore and went to the front porch. With Kurry on my lap, I began, pretending that life really was the way Bert and Nan found it—one good time after another and nothing ever going very wrong. When it was time for lunch, I put a marker in my place so I could begin again quickly just where I'd left off.

My father was still not home from the hospital.

I had left the seashore and was in the Great West when my father finally came home in the late afternoon. He looked tired.

"She has phlebitis in both legs," he said. "That means she has a clot in the veins so that her legs swell up. She may have to stay in bed a long time."

"What about her middle? Lin Nai-Nai says there's something wrong with her middle."

My father sighed as if he wished Lin Nai-Nai had kept still. "The doctor thinks that is going to be all right."

"Can I see her?"

"Not for a day or two." My father lay down on the sofa and fell right to sleep.

The next day I stayed glued to the Bobbsey Twins. I was glad that there were so many books. I was glad that I didn't have to worry about how any of them would turn out. When my father came back from the hospital, I kept my finger in my place.

"How is she?" I asked.

"She's doing all right." He spoke in a strong voice and smiled as he sat down on the top step of the porch. "And I have a surprise for you."

I closed the book. "Animal, vegetable, or mineral?"

He laughed. "Animal," he said. "Jean, you have a baby sister."

I heard the words all right but they seemed to dangle in the air. I couldn't make them travel all the way into my head.

"Are you joking?" I whispered.

"No, I'm not joking. You have a baby sister."

The word "baby" registered first. "A boy or a girl?" I asked and then the whole sentence hit me. I threw the Bobbsey Twins into the air so they landed in a jumble, pages topsy-turvy. "I have a baby sister," I yelled. I jumped up and threw myself at my father. "I have a baby sister." It was the most wonderful sentence I had ever heard. I ran inside and told Mrs. Jordan. "I have a baby sister." I ran to Lin Nai-Nai's room. "I have a baby sister." I went back to the porch where both Mr. and Mrs. Jordan had joined my father.

"What does she look like?"

"Small," my father said. "Brown hair like you. She was born six weeks early but the doctor says she'll be fine."

Suddenly I realized that my mother and father had known about this baby for a long time. Probably everyone had known but me.

"Why didn't you tell me before?" I asked.

"Mother was having a hard time," my father said. "She didn't want you to worry."

"Did Mrs. Hull know?"

"Yes. Mother told Mrs. Hull."

So Andrea had known too and had probably been told not to tell. But how could I not have noticed? I asked myself. How could I not have seen what was going on under those loose dresses? There was part of me that might have felt cross but I couldn't feel cross today.

There wasn't room in me for anything but a wild, tumbling excitement. Just think, I told myself, I would never be alone again. There'd always be another child in the family. Of course there'd be eleven years between us, but my father had a sister, my Aunt Margaret, who was twenty years younger than he was. Who cared about age? I had a sister, oh, I had a sister!

"When can I see her?"

"Tomorrow, I think," my father said.

I couldn't stay still. I raced up the hill in the sunshine, my heart singing. When I ran out of breath, I threw myself down on the grass and before I knew it, I had begun a new picture album. Me reading to my sister. Me walking her to kindergarten the first day of school. Me picking her up when she fell down. And the older she grew, the more we would share.

The next afternoon when I walked down the hill to the hospital with my father, I carried two bunches of daisies, one for my mother, one for my sister.

"Now that the baby has been born," my father said, "we think the worst is over for Mother. But until her legs get well, she'll have to stay in the hospital. Maybe for most of the summer. If she's coming along all right, I'll be going back to Hankow next week for a while."

"Well, I'll visit her," I said. "Every day."

"Yes. You and Mrs. Jordan can go together. Or you and Lin Nai-Nai. But I want you to remember one thing. You mustn't worry Mother. If something goes wrong or if you don't feel well, just don't mention it. We want her to get well fast. All right?"

"All right."

We went to see the baby first. She was in a basket in the doctor's office where he could keep an eye on her. He got up from his desk, all smiles. "She's doing just fine," he said.

She was tiny. And kind of puckered-looking, the way your hands get if they've been in the water a long time, but I knew this was just because she was new. Her hands were folded into two little fists and when I slipped a finger into her fist, she held on. "I'm your sister," I said. Even if she couldn't understand, I wanted to tell her. "I'm your sister, Jean." I put the daisies in a glass beside the basket.

Then we went to see my mother. She smiled when she saw me and held out her hand. "How do you like your sister?" she asked.

"I think she's the most wonderful baby in the whole world."

"We'll have to think of a name for her before your father goes back to Hankow."

Of course I had already decided what her name should be, but I remembered I wasn't supposed to upset my mother. I waited until the Jordans and my father and I were sitting at the supper table.

"I think she should be named Marjorie," I announced.

My father was cutting up his meat. "I don't believe Mother would like that," he said. "You have to think how the first name goes with the last name. Marjorie Guttery. That doesn't sound nice."

"I think it does."

"We've talked about a few names. Ann. Ruth."

I shook my head. "Too short. Like mine, they're both too short."

Every time I saw the baby in the next few days, I thought she looked more and more like a Marjorie, but I knew that was a lost cause. All I hoped was that whatever they called her, she wouldn't sound too good. I didn't want a sister who would be one-hundred-percent perfect.

The night before he left for Hankow, my father told us it was decided. My mother had picked the name.

Miriam.

Straight out of the Bible, I thought. A name for a saint.

"I hate it," I said.

My father looked at me over the rim of his coffee cup. "Well, don't tell Mother."

"Do you want me to lie?"

"I think you're smart enough," he said, "to make her happy without actually telling a lie."

After my father had gone the next day, I went to the hospital with Mrs. Jordan.

"How do you like the baby's name?" my mother asked.

"I think it's a nice Bible name," I said primly.

My mother turned to Mrs. Jordan. "Has Jean been good?" she asked. Now that my father had left, I knew that my mother was worried that I'd be a bother to Mrs. Jordan. I knew that every time we visited, my mother would ask the same question. "Has Jean been good? Has Jean been good?" All summer long. I felt like a coolie who has had a load strapped to his back before going up the mountain.

Later while Mrs. Jordan was talking to the doctor in the hall, I slipped into his office for a private visit with my sister. Someday, I thought, she'd have a load on her back too.

"Listen," I told her, "I don't care what your name is, I just want you to know that I'm not going to worry about your being good. And don't expect too much of me either. We're together, remember. We're sisters." I could hardly wait for her to understand.

My life took on a pattern now. Since I could never stay long at the hospital, there was a lot of time to fill up. Mrs. Jordan introduced me to some other children, and when I wasn't reading in my window seat with Kurry or writing letters at my blue desk, I was often with Peggy Reynolds who lived two houses down. We played tennis and checkers and I lent her the Bobbsey Twins and she lent me the Rosemary books. Once the Jordans took me to the Cave of the Immortals in the West Valley. At the temple inside the cave, I could go up to the altar and talk to the Rain God if I wanted to, but I didn't have a thing to say to him. My prayers had nothing to do with weather.

What I really liked best that summer was going on little breakfast picnics with Lin Nai-Nai. We had found a fish pool in a park not too far away and while the fog was still lifting from the ground, we would sit there in the midst of bluebells and tiger lilies and eat our hard-boiled eggs and bananas and drink the tea we'd brought in a thermos bottle. Sometimes I gave Lin Nai-Nai English lessons while we ate. She could carry on a conversation now about health and one about weather, but she couldn't manage to say "Miriam." So we settled on Mei Mei, the Chinese word for Little Sister, which I liked better anyway.

After three weeks, my father came back, but he could only stay for a few days. We went down together to the hospital and found Mother sitting up in a chair, her legs propped on a stool. The baby had been moved into her room. Miriam had lost her pucker now and when she looked at me, I imagined she knew who I was.

"She had her fingernails cut yesterday," my mother said.

That was wonderful news, I thought. If her fingernails were growing, the rest of her must be hurrying up too. I leaned over the basket to see.

"Would you like to hold her?" my mother said.

I had never supposed that they would trust me to hold her. I sat in a chair and my father placed her gently in my arms. She didn't cry. She just looked up at me and I looked down at her. I'm so lucky, I thought. Who would have dreamed I would be so lucky?

When I went back to the house, I told Lin Nai-Nai about it. The next morning at breakfast I was telling the Jordans when one of the servants came in with a note and gave it to my father. He tore it open and as he read, his shoulders slumped. When he looked up from the note, there was emptiness in his eyes.

"Miriam died last night," he said. "They don't know exactly why." He pushed back his chair. "I must go right down to the hospital."

I didn't recognize my voice when I spoke. "Will you tell Mother?"

"She knows."

"But I thought—" I didn't go on. I thought something awful would happen to my mother if she were even a little bit upset. I was afraid that now she might break in two. Mr. Jordan went out of the house with my father and Mrs. Jordan put her arms around me. I think she expected me to cry, but I didn't feel like crying. I felt numb. Wooden. Oh, I should have known, I told myself. It was too good to be true. I should have known.

Later that morning my father took me to see Mother. She was lying white-faced in bed and she put up her arms to hug me, but she didn't say a word about Miriam. It seemed to me that I would never dare say Miriam's name to my mother for fear of what it might do to her.

In the afternoon Lin Nai-Nai came to me with a little picnic basket in her hand. "We'll go to the bluebells," she said. "That will be good for you."

Still wooden, I followed her. We sat down by the pool and she spread out the picnic. Almond cookies too—my favorite. I tried to eat but I couldn't.

"Cry," Lin Nai-Nai said. "Put your head down," she patted her lap, "and cry. It's the only way."

"I don't feel like crying. I don't feel anything." But suddenly I did feel. Not grief. Anger. It flooded through me. I was furious. At first I couldn't figure out whom I was furious with, but then I knew. I was mad at Dr. Carhart. I picked a daisy and began ripping off the petals. Who did he think he was? What did he know? Standing up in a pulpit and saying death was a glory! Nothing to be sad about! What kind of glory could it be for a little baby who wouldn't know if she was in a dark tunnel or not? I took a bite of hard-boiled egg and chewed it furiously. I ate my whole lunch that way. In a rage. Then we went back to the house.

That night I tried to write to my grandmother but no words came. It would be weeks and weeks before she'd know that Miriam had died. In fact, she was probably still getting used to her being born. She was still happy. I crumpled the paper.

We had a funeral for Miriam in the living room. My mother couldn't leave the hospital, of course, but my father and the Jordans had invited a few friends. The tiny white coffin was set on a table. There was a wreath of flowers on it but no bluebells. I ran out and picked some bluebells and put them in the center of the wreath before the service started. We sang hymns but I didn't sing. There was no song in me. The minister from the Kuling church read the twenty-fourth psalm and said a prayer, but he didn't mention glory, thank goodness. Then because Miriam was to be buried in Hankow, two coolies carried the little coffin down the long narrow path. Standing alone with my father on the porch, I thought I had never seen anything as sad as that tiny coffin winding down that steep mountain, bumping along under two poles that the coolies carried on their shoulders. Every bump was another *never*. Never, never, never, never.

When the coffin was out of sight, my father put his arm around me. "You know, Jean," he said, "you have been very, very good through this."

Suddenly something inside me exploded. I wheeled around at my father. "Good!" I shouted. "That's all anyone can think about. Good! I haven't even thought about being good. I haven't tried to be good. I don't care about being good. I have just been *me*. Doesn't anyone ever look at *me*?"

My father had sat down in a rocking chair and had pulled me onto his lap. I was crying now. All those tears that had been stored up inside were pouring out. My whole body was shaking with them. My father held me close and rocked back and forth.

"You don't understand," I cried. "You and Mother will never understand. I was waiting for Miriam to grow. I knew she'd understand. She was the only one. I was counting on her. I *needed* her."

I looked up at my father. His head was back on the headrest, his eyes were closed. Tears were streaming down his cheeks. "I do understand, Jean," he said. And we went on rocking and rocking together.

4

After my father left this time for Hankow, he didn't come back at all. Communist soldiers had begun to attack Wuchang (the city across the river from Hankow) and he was helping to set up hospitals for the sick and wounded. He wrote that we should come home as soon as Mother was able in case the riverboats stopped running, so in the middle of September, even though Mother could walk only a little, we went back down the mountain. Kurry was shut up tight in a basket on my lap, and the Jordans, who were traveling all the way to Hankow with us, led our procession.

I wasn't sorry to leave Kuling. The bluebells and the tiger lilies had dried up and dropped off their stems. And I was glad to get away from the wind. Every night it came howling down from the mountaintop as if it were looking for something lost. It shook the trees inside out, rattled at doors, banged at shutters. Then it would stop for breath. Not there, it seemed to say. Not there. Then it would begin again. *Whooo, whooo,* going back to all the same places it had been, looking and looking. Some nights it never gave up. Even in a war, I thought, I would be safer in Hankow than in these mountains and with a wind that might, for all I knew, be looking for me. Maybe in Hankow my mother would get well quickly so I wouldn't have to worry about upsetting her. Maybe sometime I could talk out loud

about once having had a real baby sister with fingernails that had to be cut.

Not yet, of course. My mother was carried down the
mountain on a stretcher, and although she got up for
meals on the boat, she spent most of the time lying
down in our cabin. When we approached Hankow, she
went on deck and stretched out on a long chair.

"It looks just the same, doesn't it?" she said.

And it did. Even from the middle of the river I could
see the plane trees marching up the Bund in their white
socks. (Their socks were painted on to keep bugs away,
my father said.) As we came closer, I saw that there
were more coolies on the dock than usual, more jostling, more noise, but I thought nothing of it. Just coolies. There was nothing that looked like war.

Then the gangplank was lowered and my father
bounded on the deck in his white panama hat and his
white duck suit. He hugged us both, but Mother got the
first hug and the longer one because of course she was
the one to worry about. He shook hands with the Jordans. "This may be the last boat to get through," he
announced triumphantly. My father loved to set
records: to be the last, the first, the fastest, to get
through what he called Narrow Squeaks.

He explained that he'd borrowed the Hulls' Dodge
sedan (which the Y.M.C.A. had bought) and parked it
close by on the Bund. Did my mother think she could
walk that far?

It really wasn't far and when my mother said yes, she
could, my father motioned for coolies to carry our luggage to the car. I think he suspected there might be
trouble because he stood on the gangplank and held up
four fingers, as if he were trying to keep more coolies
from coming on board. Mr. Jordan, a wide man,

blocked the gangplank by standing right behind my father.

But suddenly there was a roar from the dock and thirty or more coolies stormed up the gangplank, lifted my father and Mr. Jordan right off their feet and set them down on the deck. They circled around our pile of luggage (ten pieces), shouting, grabbing up suitcases and bundles, even pulling the briefcase out of my father's hand. One coolie, seeing the basket I was holding, tried to pull it away. I clung tight.

"This is not baggage," I shouted. "It's alive." When he didn't let go, I kicked him on the shin. "It's a baby tiger!" I yelled. The coolie glanced at a tall, pock-marked man who stood at the edge of the crowd, each hand tucked, Chinese fashion, up his other sleeve. He was better dressed than the coolies and seemed to be the boss. He motioned for the coolie to leave me alone.

By this time five coolies had taken charge of the baggage. The others had backed off but had not left the boat. "Pay now," they shouted. "Make the foreign devils pay now." The tall, pockmarked man unfolded his arms; in one hand he held a knife.

The cost of carrying a bag had always been five coppers, so for eleven bags (including the briefcase), the total should have been fifty-five cents. Today my father handed a twenty-cent piece to each of the five coolies which was, of course, almost double the normal rate.

"I know you fellows are having hard times," my father said.

The coolies threw the money on the deck as if it were dirt. All the coolies began chanting: "Fifty cents a bag! Fifty cents! Fifty cents!"

I could see my father set his chin in his stubborn,

not-giving-in way. Then he glanced at my mother and without another word he opened his wallet and pulled out five single dollars, one for each coolie and an extra fifty cents for the man with the briefcase.

As we followed the coolies off the boat, I thought the trouble was over. Some of the coolies lost interest when we reached the dock and went their own way, but some, including the boss, stayed with us. When we reached the stone steps that led to the Bund, the five coolies plunked the baggage down. That was as far as they went for a dollar, they said. They each needed two dollars more to finish the job.

My father's chin turned hard as stone. He looked at the boss. "We will go on," he said, "or I will call the police." He raised his arm as if he were about to call the police, but the boss pointed his knife at him. Other coolies produced knives.

"If you call the police," the boss said, "you will be dead by the time they get here."

I felt my knees go weak and tremble. I was surprised, because I didn't know that people's knees really shook when they were scared. I had supposed that writers of books just said that in the same way as they made happy endings at the last minute. As I looked at my father's chin and at the men with their knives, I knew no one was going to give in. Only a writer could save us now, I thought.

Suddenly Lin Nai-Nai nudged me and pointed to the Bund which as usual was lined with rickshas parked on both sides of the street, but there were no coolies with the rickshas. All of them, up and down the street, were running toward us. In a moment they had surrounded us.

"This way, Mr. Gau. Hurry. This way," one of the

coolies cried. I recognized him. My father had helped him once when he was in trouble and he'd been our friend ever since. He must have seen what was going on and called the others. Forming a double line that led to the Dodge sedan, they hurried us and our baggage into the car while they stood guard. My father and the Jordans slid into the front seat, my mother, Lin Nai-Nai, and I into the back. The ricksha coolies stayed until we had the car started and were off the street. It was a grand rescue. I didn't think there was a writer in the whole world who could have done better.

But I was afraid something terrible might have happened to my mother. My father and the Jordans were all asking how she was and she said she was all right and she did seem to be. I put my hand on her knees and they weren't even shaking. Maybe she was better already.

As soon as we were inside the house, I let poor Kurry out of her basket and we all gave a big sigh, glad to be safe again.

My father leaned against the door. "Well," he said proudly, "that was a Narrow Squeak!" Probably he was already thinking what a good story this would make when he wrote home, but I planned to write first.

Dear Grandma (I would say): We were almost murdered tonight but in the nick of time we were saved by a bunch of ricksha coolies. I was so scared that my knees were shaking, but don't worry about us. Just remember that in China there are always ricksha coolies around.

We went into the living room where my mother stretched out on the sofa and my father began talking about what had been going on in Hankow. Since the Jordans were leaving the next day, he wanted them to hear everything, so he went on and on, the way he did when he was taking Dr. Carhart's place and preaching a sermon. I paid no attention; it was just more Chinese-fighting talk. Who was going to rule China. Who was going to beat whom. It was like a Victrola record that had been playing ever since I was born. Then suddenly my father interrupted the record to speak to me.

"You'll be interested in this news, Jean," he said. "The British School is not going to open this fall and Miss Williams has gone back to England."

"You're joking!" I cried.

"Cross my heart," my father said.

Like all good news, it was hard to believe. I tried to imagine it. No more Miss Williams ever. No more worrying about Ian Forbes or the king of England or prisoner's base.

"We'll have lessons together," my mother said.

I nodded, thinking how I'd study my favorite subjects: poetry and George Washington and the map of America. No complicated math problems, no French. My mother didn't speak French and I had never seen her do anything but add and subtract in her account book. She said we wouldn't start for two or three weeks to give her a chance to rest.

I began to see that this war was going to mean more than just talk, but at first I didn't connect Yang Sze-Fu's fingernails with the war. Of course I was surprised the next morning when I noticed that the long, spiky nails on his pinkies were gone and were now the same length as his other nails.

I asked Lin Nai-Nai. "How come Yang Sze-Fu cut his nails?"

"He's a Communist," Lin Nai-Nai said. "Communists don't believe in long fingernails. They believe all people should be working people, no one pretending to be better than anyone else."

"Are you still interested in being a Communist?" I asked.

"No," she said. "How can I like the Communists when they are attacking my city?"

I had forgotten that Lin Nai-Nai's family lived in Wuchang. Once long ago she had explained to me that she had disgraced her family when she had run away from her husband and they would never want to see her again. Now she was worried about them, and no wonder. My father had told me how Communist soldiers were trying to make the city of Wuchang surrender by starving it to death. It was a city with walls around it, and since the soldiers wouldn't let anyone in or out, eventually the people would run out of food. I had read about sieges like this in my English history book, but in ancient days soldiers had worn armor and ridden horseback and used battering rams against the city walls. These soldiers had only cloth caps and cotton clothes, but they had a cannon which they fired from the hills and they had bombs which they dropped on the city from the one airplane they owned. And they waited.

I took Lin Nai-Nai's hand as she sat in her embroidery chair. "How many brothers and sisters do you have?" I asked.

"Two brothers. One, ten years—Dee Dee. One, twenty-two. Two sisters, sixteen and twenty, but maybe they are married now and moved away. Maybe my parents are dead. Who knows? One thing is sure, anyone alive in Wuchang is hungry."

From that moment the whole war became for me a war against Lin Nai-Nai's family. When I heard the cannon being fired across the river, I thought of Lin Nai-Nai's little brother, Dee Dee, and wondered if his knees were shaking. The first time the Communist airplane flew over Hankow on its way to Wuchang, I ran outside and shook my fist at the pilot and shouted all the Chinese swear words I knew. My mother called me in.

"What would people think if they heard you?" she asked.

"They'd think I was mad at the Communists."

"They'd think you hadn't been brought up right. And I think we'd better start lessons pretty soon."

But we didn't start right away and meanwhile I began to worry about Yang Sze-Fu being a Communist. I couldn't help seeing how he had changed. No butter pagodas now. He just slapped butter on a plate any old way and didn't even try to make our company meals special. He acted as if he hated foreigners, especially me. Sometimes he pretended he didn't hear me when I asked for cocoa.

"I think my father should fire Yang Sze-Fu," I told Lin Nai-Nai, but she shook her head.

"That would be wrong. Then he might become dangerous. He may be rude now, but no foreigners have been harmed by their servants."

But I wasn't so sure about Yang Sze-Fu. One day as I was finishing a bowl of canned cherries, I saw a drop of red at the bottom of my bowl that didn't look one bit like cherry juice. It looked like potassium. In strawberry season we used potassium to kill the germs on fresh berries. Of course before we ate them, we had to wash the potassium off with sterile water because potassium was poisonous. (In China we had to be very careful about germs.) I knew we had potassium in the kitchen and suddenly I knew that if I were writing a story about a Communist cook, I'd have him poison his foreign employers with potassium. The more I thought of it, the more sure I was that was exactly what Yang Sze-Fu was trying to do, so when no one was looking, I spit the cherries I still had in my mouth into my big linen napkin. After that, every meal I picked over my food, looking for traces of red, and sometimes with my mouth full, I'd suddenly get the feeling that I tasted potassium and I'd spit into my napkin again.

After a few days the serving boy, who took care of the napkins, spoke to Lin Nai-Nai about it and Lin Nai-Nai asked me. We were sitting beside the embroidery window.

"Oh, it's nothing," I said. I didn't want her to tell Mother. Grown-ups generally took the truth too seriously or not seriously enough; either way it meant trouble.

"Are you sick?" Lin Nai-Nai asked.

"No. It's just that sometimes when I think about the people in Wuchang, I don't want to swallow my food. I won't do it anymore, so don't tell." I was ashamed of myself for lying, so I ran out of the room to find Kurry who was a comfort to me in my guilty times. She'd purr and blink her eyes as if she were saying, "What's the difference?"

But although I looked all over the house, I couldn't find Kurry. I was always afraid that she'd streak out the front door sometime when it was open, and even though this was Hankow, not Wuchang, I didn't want her outside. (In Wuchang there were no dogs or cats left, my father said; they'd all been eaten.) She was allowed, however, in the enclosed courtyard between the house and the servants' quarters, and when I looked out the glass window in the back door, I saw her in the courtyard, crouching between Yang Sze-Fu and the serving boy, eating from a blue rice bowl. I was the one who fed Kurry. Why was she eating with the servants? More important, *what* was she eating?

I stood still and watched. The two men were squatting on their heels, eating their evening meal, shoveling rice into their mouths with chopsticks, dipping into the large bowl of vegetables and meat that sat between them. Every once in a while Yang Sze-Fu would pick up a bite and drop it into Kurry's bowl. Once he laid down his chopsticks and stroked Kurry on the head and talked to her.

Before the summer I had often squatted in the courtyard with the servants while they ate, so I went out now and joined them.

Yang Sze-Fu seemed embarrassed. "The cat likes Chinese food," he explained.

"You like my cat?" I asked.

He shrugged. "A cat is a cat. There are no foreign cats, no Chinese cats, no capitalist cats, no Communist cats. Just cats."

He picked up a cup of tea and took a loud sip from it. I noticed how, as he held the cup, he tried to hide his pinkie, and I remembered how he used to flourish it as if he felt especially superior when he was drinking tea. Suddenly I saw that no matter how strong a Communist Yang Sze-Fu was, he missed his nails and I felt sorry for him. I decided not to worry about potassium anymore.

When my father came home in the evenings now, the first thing he did was to announce how long the siege had been going on. The twenty-third day, the twenty-fourth day. It was as if this was the only way he could keep track of time. Then he would tell us the news. Sometimes the Communists had allowed a few boat-loads of sick and wounded to cross the river to hospitals that the Y.M.C.A. had helped to set up. These refugees had terrible stories to tell: houses destroyed, people sleeping in the streets, children dying, water running

low, disease spreading. I listened now because this was Lin Nai-Nai's war and I wanted it to be over. Already I was helping Lin Nai-Nai fill baskets with food to take to Wuchang as soon as the city gates opened. She knew her family might refuse to see her, but she had to try, she said. I bought a big bar of milk chocolate for her little brother, but I didn't always tell her the news that my father brought home.

Sometimes the news was so bad that my father wouldn't even tell us. Instead, he'd go to the piano and pound out the one piece he knew by heart, "Napoleon's Last Charge." I loved the piece, but even more, I liked to watch what it did to my father. He could sit down at the piano, looking as if he had given up on China, but pretty soon his left hand would get the cannon booming and the drums beating. His right hand would say Giddyap to the horses and off they'd go, galloping off to battle. Then both hands would charge faster and faster up and down the keyboard, armor clashing, bugles blowing, and by the end, I knew it didn't matter whether Napoleon ever fought again or not. My father had won.

Still the siege went on. One night at supper I tried to imagine what people in Washington, P.A., talked about at the end of the day.

"What do you suppose they think is news?" I asked.

"Well, they're probably worrying about the first frost now and wondering if they should cover up their tomatoes," my father said.

We all laughed. Suddenly it seemed both wonderful and funny to have nothing more than a frost to worry about.

"Can you imagine us when we get to Washington, P.A.?" I asked.

My father tipped his chair back. "I suppose I'll be watching the papers to see how Pittsburgh is doing in baseball."

"And Blanche and I will be talking about the length of our skirts," my mother added.

"And I'll be roller skating all over the place."

It wouldn't be long now, I thought. We were due to go to America on the twenty-sixth of April and this was the first of October. I counted on my fingers. "Just six more months," I said. "Plus a couple of weeks."

My father brought his chair down slowly. "We hope," he said.

"What do you mean—*hope*?" The date of our going back to America had always been a sure thing. We had our reservations. We knew the name of our ship, the *President Taft*. We had even bought a Dodge car that would be waiting for us in San Francisco so we could drive across the continent to Pennsylvania.

"Well, Jean," my father said, "you can see what war is like. If we were scheduled to leave Hankow next week, for instance, we couldn't do it. I'm needed here."

"But the siege will be over long before spring," I pointed out. "You said yourself you didn't think that Wuchang could hold out much longer."

"Yes, and then we'll have to take care of the people, the living and the dead." But that wasn't all, I found out. Even after Wuchang had fallen, the war wouldn't be over. This was only what my father called a "skirmish." The main part of the Nationalist Army hadn't even arrived.

"Well, for heaven's sake," I exploded, "you don't expect to hang around China until it's all through fighting, do you?"

"No. I expect we'll go to America on schedule. I just thought I'd warn you. Delay is possible."

I should know by this time, I thought, that nothing in the world was sure. Certainly nothing on this side of the world. I felt the tears beginning when Mother put her hand over mine.

"We're going to begin lessons tomorrow morning," she said. "So get your pencils sharpened and your desk in order. School begins at nine o'clock."

My mother was really much better. She was up for most of the day now and her keys hung around her waist, which meant that she was back in charge. (I envied her the keys: desk drawer keys, kitchen cupboard keys, trunk keys, door keys. Foreigners locked up everything.) She was even well enough so that we had visited friends, which was a treat. Since I wasn't allowed out alone now, days often became boring and I was glad that we'd be starting lessons and I thought my mother must be glad too. She had been a Latin teacher before she was married and my father said she'd been a whiz-bang.

We began school on the thirty-first day of the siege. I had my pencils, razor-sharp, lined up on my desk with a red pencil for my mother to use for marking papers. I had put a little bell on the desk so she could ring it when a class was over or when it was time for recess. I thought it would be like play-school. Of course I expected to work, but I thought we'd have fun pretending to be teacher and pupil when we were really mother and daughter.

I guess I hadn't understood what it meant to be a whiz-bang. My mother started right off with complicated arithmetic, and since she didn't know French, she said she would teach me Latin.

"Latin?" I cried. "No one in America studies Latin until they're in high school. You said so yourself. You were a high school teacher."

"So you'll have a head start." I could see my mother wasn't pretending anything. Even her voice became the kind of teacher voice you didn't argue with. So I learned about dative and ablative cases and I solved problems about how long it would take a train to go from Hankow to Peking if it were going so many miles an hour and stopped five times on the way. I knew that grown-ups never figured out such problems; they just looked at timetables. But when I pointed this out to my mother, she said someone had to make up the time-tables. It didn't make a bit of difference that I intended to write stories, not timetables, when I grew up.

Of course I liked some subjects more than others. I learned the capitals of all forty-eight states, and when my mother called out the name of the state, I snapped back the name of the city. I liked reading about explorers planting flags all over the New World and I marveled how they never looked mussed up in their pictures, although I thought exploring must be dirty work. But there was Balboa taking possession of the Pacific Ocean and he was neat as a pin. Still, the best part of every day was when my mother rang the bell which meant that school was over and she could be my mother again.

On the fortieth day (October 10, 1926) the siege was over and my mother declared a school holiday. Lin Nai-Nai and I went to the market to buy fresh food for her baskets because she expected to go to Wuchang the next day with my father. As a member of the relief committee, my father was already there and would be going back and forth for a long time, I supposed.

But when my father came home that night, he looked too sick to go anywhere. He said he wasn't sure if he could even eat supper. As he lowered himself into a chair in the living room, he just shook his head.

"You can't imagine it," he told my mother. I think he'd forgotten I was in the room or he might not have told all that he did. So many dead rotting bodies in the streets! In just one hour he'd counted sixty bodies being wheeled through the city gates in wheelbarrows. "And I figure there are at least fifty thousand sick people that will have to be brought to Hankow." His voice cracked as he spoke, and I guessed he was thinking about sights too pitiful to put into words.

"A bomb went through the roof of the Wuchang Y.M.C.A. building," he went on, "but they continued to give out free rice as long as they had it."

Part of my father still seemed to be in Wuchang, which must have been why he looked so sick and why he didn't seem to hear the knock on the living-room door.

My mother called, "Come in," and there was Lin Nai-Nai.

"Excuse me, Mr. Gau," she said, "but you promised that I might go to Wuchang with you. What time should I be ready tomorrow?"

It was my mother who answered. "Oh, Lin Nai-Nai," she said, "I think you should wait a couple of days until the city has been cleaned up a little."

Lin Nai-Nai stood firm on her little bound feet. "If my family are hungry, they are hungry now."

My father dragged himself back from wherever he'd been, looked at Lin Nai-Nai, and nodded. He told her to be ready at seven o'clock. They would cross the river in the relief committee's launch and he would see that she got as far as the Wuchang "Y." He knew she hoped to stay for a while with her family—that is, if they'd let her.

"Leave a message for me at the 'Y,' " he said, "so we'll know your plans. And when you're ready to return, I'll arrange for it." He pulled out his wallet. "You'll need some money."

The next morning after my father and Lin Nai-Nai had left, my mother suddenly announced that we'd have another school holiday.

"Let's go visiting," she said.

"Not to the Gales'," I begged. Mr. Gale owned the Dodge agency and Mrs. Gale was my mother's best friend. They had no children but they did have two pet monkeys, Nip and Tuck—disgusting creatures who should have been left in the jungle. They were not housebroken, but for some reason Mrs. Gale thought she was doing me a favor when she dropped one in my lap for me to play with.

"All right," my mother agreed. "How about the Littles in the Episcopalian Mission?"

It was a good choice, one of the few places where I still had friends. Many families had left Hankow and many had sent their children away for their education—to boarding school in Shanghai or to relatives back home in England or America—but at the Episcopalian Mission there were three girls, Nancy Little, Margaret Masters, and Isobel Wilbur, all a little younger but I didn't mind that. What I liked was that there was space to play in the center of their circle of houses. Trees and grass and swings.

When my mother went inside to visit with Mrs. Little, Nancy and I ran to the swings. And how I ran! It was as if my legs had been holding back and holding back without my knowing it. I jumped on a swing and pumped myself right up to the sky. Margaret and Isobel came out and we played tag and climbed trees and shouted until we were out of breath and then we threw ourselves down on Nancy's porch.

We lay there panting for a few minutes and suddenly I heard myself say something I had not planned to say at all.

"Did you know I had a baby sister this summer?" I asked.

Nancy sat up and handed me a piece of gum. "Yeah, I heard."

"If she had lived," I said, "she would be four months old now."

"You keep track?" Nancy was pulling the chewed gum from her mouth and stretching it out with both hands so that it was a flat, rubbery piece punctured with holes. "These are Miss Williams' pants," she laughed.

I didn't want to talk about Miss Williams. "Sure, I keep track," I said. "I know the exact day she would have turned four months."

Nancy stuffed the gum back into her mouth. "Well, let me tell you. Four-month-old babies are a pain in the neck. I know. We've had two."

My mother came out on the porch with a sweater for me to put on. I don't know what got into me but I had started something I didn't want to let go.

"I was just telling everyone about Miriam," I said. "How she would have been four months old now."

My mother looked as if I'd slapped her in the face. She didn't say a word, but as she went back into the house, I knew she would never in her whole life talk about Miriam. It was as if I'd never had a baby sister.

I stretched my gum out the way Nancy had, only I

pulled mine so thin it was almost all holes. "These are your pants," I said and I ran back to the swings.

When we got home at about four o'clock, my mother went upstairs to take her afternoon rest. I went into the living room where Wong Sze-Fu was dusting the furniture with a feather duster. He swooped the feathers over the piano keys and as the dust drifted back down, he told me that Lin Nai-Nai was home. She had come about a half hour ago.

Already! But my father wasn't even home!

I ran to the servants' quarters and up to her room. I was so worried that I didn't even knock, just slipped inside. Her back was turned toward me as she sat in a straight chair, swaying to and fro. "Ai-ya," she whispered. "Ai-ya, ai-ya." Her trouser legs were rolled up. The strips of bandage that bound her feet had been taken off and her stumps of feet, hard little hooves with the toes bent under, were soaking in a pan of water on the floor. "Ai-ya," she said.

I threw myself on my knees beside her chair and put my arms around her waist. "What is it?" I whispered. "What happened?"

I had never seen her feet unbound or tears on her face or her sleek black hair straggling out of the bun on the back of her neck. She put an arm around my shoulder as if she welcomed me, as if good friends were supposed to share bad times.

"My father would not allow me in the house," she said. "My mother is sick but he wouldn't let me see her. He would not even take the food. He closed the door in my face."

With her eyes shut, Lin Nai-Nai shook her head back and forth as if the world were more than she could understand.

"I just left the baskets on the doorstep and ran. I ran

all the way to the river and rented a sampan to take me across. Then I walked from the Bund."

"Oh, your poor, poor feet," I moaned.

"Yes, my poor feet."

She was quiet for a moment but I knew she had more to tell. "I saw Dee Dee," she went on. "He is the only one home and he is thin. So thin. My sisters are married and in Shanghai. My other brother was killed by a shell." She shut her eyes again.

"Dee Dee told you that?"

"Yes. He ran after me in the street. He told me that when he grows up, I can live with him." She shook her head. "He doesn't know that when he grows up, he will be a man. A different person. Now he is still a boy and when I told him there was chocolate in the basket, he forgot everything else. And when he left, I began running again." She made a small laugh. "Bound feet running. Like a stumbling duck."

I tried to think of something to say that would make Lin Nai-Nai feel better, but I could find nothing. As far as I could see, she had not a single thing in her life to look forward to.

"I'll make you a cup of tea." I went to her little two-burner stove and put water on to boil. When the tea was ready, she drank noisily to show her appreciation. Tomorrow she would feel better, she said. I shouldn't worry.

But I didn't see how she would feel better. That night at supper I asked what would happen to Lin Nai-Nai when we went back to America.

"She'll go to live with Mr. and Mrs. T. K. Hu," my mother said. "We made arrangements months ago, but of course she hoped to go back to her family. Since she can't, I'm sure she'll be happy with the Hus."

Still, I couldn't bear to think of leaving Lin Nai-Nai.

"How will we ever know what's happening to each other?" I asked her one day. "You can't write English and I can't read Chinese."

"Mr. Hu can write for me and he can read your letters to me. You can tell me all about your grandmother and how you feed the chickens and how happy you are."

As much as I'd talked, I found it hard to imagine myself actually picking up a pen to write such a letter. Ever since my father had said delay was possible, I hadn't dared to make plans for fear of being disappointed. I had tried to put America right out of my mind. Of course I wrote to my grandmother as usual and we sent off our Christmas packages to Washington, P.A., but I wasn't keeping any album of pictures of what it would be like when we got there. I held out until Christmas and then I couldn't hold out any longer.

It all started when I opened the present from my father. It was a big, soft package and inside there was blue-and-gray-plaid wool that looked like a blanket, but it was not a regular blanket, my father said. It was a steamer rug made especially for ocean voyages. He described how I would sit on a deck chair as we crossed the Pacific and I'd cover myself with the steamer rug and while I looked at the ocean, a steward would bring me a cup of beef tea. That did it. How could I stay put in China when my steamer rug was ready for the high seas?

Then I opened my grandmother's present. Of course she sent me a petticoat but she also sent a calendar for the next year: 1927. She had attached a note: "I have a calendar just like this. Beginning January 1st, let's both cross off the days until you're home. That will make the time go faster." She figured that it might be July by the time we had crossed the continent, so at the end of every month she had written down how many days were left. At the end of January: 150 days. At the end of February: 122 days. As I turned the pages, the days seemed to fly past. Then I came to July, and there pasted over the whole month was a picture of my grandmother and my grandfather and my Aunt Margaret.

My grandmother was a large woman who looked as if she did everything in a big way. In the picture, she was laughing so hard I could almost hear her, and her arms were out as if she were waiting for me to run into them. Beside her, my grandfather smiled under his mustache as if he were saying, "How about a game of horseshoes?" (My father said he was a champion.)

On the other side was my Aunt Margaret. I hadn't seen a picture of her since she'd been in high school and now she was twenty-one and taught music and had lots of beaus. I'd been afraid that maybe she had turned into a flapper with spit curls and spike heels and she might not like me. But when I saw her picture, I knew I could get in bed with her on Sunday mornings and tell jokes even if she had been out late the night before with a beau.

"Do you think we really will leave for America on time?" I asked.

"Yes," my mother said. "I feel it in my bones."

That was the best Christmas present of all. I knew that my mother's bones were almost always right.

5

In history books war seemed to be a simple matter of two sides fighting, the right side against the wrong, so I didn't see how this Chinese war was ever going to make it into history. In the first place, there weren't just two sides. There were warlords scattered around, each with his own army, and there was the Nationalist Army (under General Chiang Kai-shek) which was trying to conquer the warlords and unify the country. And there were the Communists who were supposed to be part of the Nationalist movement, but they had their own ideas, my father said, and they didn't always agree with General Chiang Kai-shek. Both the Communists and the Nationalists wanted to make things better in China, he explained, but both did terrible things to people who opposed them. If a man was an enemy, sometimes they'd cut off his head and stick it up on a pole as a warning to others. My father had seen this with his own eyes.

Furthermore, it wasn't armies who made the most trouble in Hankow. Gangs of Communist-organized workers were the ones who did the rioting. In January they took over the British concession and returned it to the Chinese. I didn't understand much of what was going on, but it didn't matter since all I cared about was going to America on time. And it looked as if we would. In February we had some of our furniture and all of our Chinese things crated for shipment. We still had our beds and chairs and bureaus and dining-room furniture, so we could get along, but even so, the house was bare and echoey. It was while we were in the midst of this packing that Mr. and Mrs. T. K. Hu came calling. Mr. Hu was carrying a large box which he handed to my father.

"Since you are packing," he said, "we thought this would be the time to give you our remembrance."

My father unwrapped the package and took out a very large ginger jar. Shiny Chinese yellow it was, the happiest color in the world, and it was decorated with bright green characters which wished us long life and health and happiness and lots of money which certainly took care of my wishes. As we stood admiring the jar, Mr. Hu took it from my father's hands and set it on one side of our fireplace.

"A pair of these jars was given us as a wedding gift," he said. "They have always stood one on each side of our fireplace. We will keep one and now you have the other. When we look at ours, we will think of you and when you look at yours, you will think of us."

My mother put her arms around Mrs. Hu. My father took one of Mr. Hu's hands in both of his. "Old friend," he said. "Old friend." He must have been misty-eyed, for he took off his glasses and wiped them. Suddenly I found myself blinking back tears and I didn't know why. I was counting the days on the calendar, wasn't I? Then how could a yellow ginger jar turn everything inside me upside down?

Mr. Hu, a large, merry-faced man whom I'd always liked, turned to me.

"And when you look at that jar, Miss Jean," he said, "you can think: 'I was born in China. Part of me will always be there.'"

I had never planned to think any such thought. I was upset by the idea and changed the subject.

"Mr. Hu," I said, "if I write letters to Lin Nai-Nai in English, will you read them to her in Chinese?"

He smiled as we all sat down. "Yes. And you can be sure that we'll take good care of your Lin Nai-Nai."

There was something else. I knew I should have talked to my mother about this first but she might have said no. "Mr. Hu," I said, "do you think you could take care of my cat too?"

"Jean!" My mother was embarrassed but before she could stop me, I scooped up Kurry who was under the sofa. "She's a gentle cat," I said.

"Of course we'll take her." Mr. Hu smiled and Mrs. Hu scratched Kurry in her favorite spot behind the ears.

Everything was going well. In March my father received word that a new man was being sent to the Y.M.C.A. to take his place, so I didn't see how my father could feel "needed" now. We planned to take the riverboat from Hankow on April 15, arriving in Shanghai on the twentieth. We would stay with the Hulls for six days before the *President Taft* sailed.

We hadn't heard from the Hulls for about a month but the last news had not been good. Mrs. Hull had written that she and Mr. Hull were going to get a divorce and he had moved to an apartment. Andrea wrote that her father was happy in his apartment and maybe this was for the best, after all. The rest of them might go to America. She didn't know when but she was ready. She had learned the Charleston.

Why would Andrea want to learn the Charleston? I wondered. That was a flapper thing to do and Andrea was only in eighth grade. I asked my mother about it.

"Andrea has always been old for her age," my mother pointed out. "She even looks older than she is." (That was true.) "And in Shanghai, Americans are crazy to keep up with American fads. They don't want to fall behind."

Well, I just hoped that Andrea hadn't grown up so much that she'd forgotten that I was to have a bathroom of my own when we visited.

On the morning of March 26 when I sat down at my desk, I crossed out March 25 on the calendar. Eighty-five days crossed out, ninety-six to go before July. But only twenty before we left for Shanghai, which was really the beginning of our trip home.

At about ten o'clock that morning as my mother was reviewing me in spelling, we heard the front door being flung open. We knew it was my father because of the way he ran up the stairs—two at a time. When he appeared at the door, he had that excited, tense look that meant a Narrow Squeak was on its way.

"All women and children have to leave Hankow today. You have about three hours to pack and get ready." He must have run home because he was still out of breath.

"What's happened?" My mother banged the spelling book shut and stood up as if she were ready to leave that very minute.

The day before yesterday the Nationalist Army had captured Nanking (down the river from Hankow), my father told us, and afterwards the soldiers had gone wild. They had broken into foreign homes, knocked foreigners around, stolen right and left. They were doing such terrible things to people that American and British gunboats had opened fire on them. Foreign gunboats hadn't done this before, my father said, and there was no telling what might happen now. There might be wholesale murder of foreigners up and down the Yangtse. We might find ourselves at war.

I could feel my knees beginning to shake. This time, however, it was not only from being scared but from being mad. Fifteen days left and this crazy war might still spoil everything.

"You'll come with us, won't you?" I asked my father. "You won't wait?" My father shook his head. This boat was for women and children. He'd take the boat on the fifteenth, if all went well.

If! There it was again. That nasty little word that was always snapping at my plans.

"Pack as many clothes as you can. Stuff it all in," my father said. "What doesn't fit, I'll bring when I come." He was already on his way to the attic to bring down suitcases and then he was going to the boat to see about our cabin. If he made arrangements for our luggage to be taken to the boat before we went, he said, we could probably avoid trouble.

My mother turned to me. "Get Lin Nai-Nai. I'll need her help."

As I started for the door, I realized that this might be my only chance to give Lin Nai-Nai my good-bye present. My father had framed a picture of Kurry and me and I had wrapped it in red tissue paper. I grabbed it out of my dresser drawer and ran to the servants' quarters.

Lin Nai-Nai was just coming out of her room. She had heard the news.

"I have a present for you," I said.

"I have one for you too." I went into her room and on her bed was a small soft present also wrapped in red tissue paper.

"You mustn't open this," she said, "until you have left China."

"On the ship?"

"Yes. After the ship has sailed."

"Well, open yours at the same time," I said. "April twenty-sixth. That way we'll almost be opening them together." I had planned a private good-bye tea party in her room with almond cookies and rice cakes. Now there wasn't time for anything. I put my arms around her. "Oh, Lin Nai-Nai," I moaned.

Back upstairs my mother was rushing from room to room, her arms full of clothes. Suitcases were open all over the beds.

"May I pack the small green suitcase just for myself?" I asked.

"Yes, but take only what you'll need from here to Shanghai. We'll repack at the Hulls'." As she handed things to Lin Nai-Nai, she would say, "Brown suitcase. Blue." Suddenly she turned back to me. "No books," she said. "But don't forget underwear. And a sweater and socks."

I had put Lin Nai-Nai's present on the bottom of my bag so I wouldn't be separated from it and now I quickly covered the two books I had packed with a bunch of underwear. On top I put everyday clothes and at the last minute I happened to think of "wholesale murder" so I stuck in some first-aid equipment.

At twelve o'clock my father returned. Everything was all set, he said. He'd made private deals with coolies whom he could trust and they were outside now.

"How do you know we won't all be mobbed as we get on the boat?" I asked.

My father waved his hand as if there were no time for silly questions. Then he went along with the baggage to see that it got on the boat. When he came back, he honked the horn on the Dodge sedan to let us know it was time to go.

"We're going to stop for the Gales," he told us as we got in the car. "They found their car this morning with four flat tires."

At the Gales' house my father honked again and out they came—Mr. and Mrs. Gale carrying a cage between them. I couldn't believe it, so I got out of the car to make sure. Yes, Nip and Tuck were inside. Chattering. Making messes.

"You're not taking them, are you?" I asked.

"Of course I'm taking them," Mrs. Gale spoke sharply. "I'm not leaving them for the Communists."

I was furious. Here I'd left a sweet, well-mannered, housebroken cat behind and they were dragging along two disgusting, smelly, flea-covered monkeys. I slid into the front seat with my mother and let the Gales and their dirty animals have the backseat to themselves. I nudged my mother and she nudged me back. She hated those monkeys too.

On the Bund gray-coated soldiers with rifles over their shoulders were stationed all over the place. They were here to keep order, my father said. They knew the gunboats would fire if they had to and they evidently didn't want that to happen. Crowds of Chinese were milling around but they didn't look like organized riot-makers, just ordinary Chinese who had come out of curiosity to laugh at the foreigners scuttling away. The Gales and their monkeys were, of course, the main attraction, and I couldn't help grinning as the crowd jeered and joked about them.

On the dock I saw that our boat had been fitted all around with huge steel plates. They were meant to stop bullets, but according to Mr. Gale, they'd been put up so clumsily, they'd fall over if a shell hit them.

"Do you really think we'll be fired on?" I asked.

My father gave me a reassuring pat. "Probably the worst thing about your trip will be that those steel plates will cut off your view. You won't be able to see a thing, so you better take a last look now."

Before going up the gangplank, I turned around and looked at Hankow. No one could say it was a pretty city but today with spring in the air, it was at its best. I tried to memorize the Bund. The American flag flying merrily over the consulate. The branches of the plane trees bumpy with buds. The clock on the Customs House looking down, like a great-uncle, on us all.

Then I noticed that not six feet away from me a little boy was jumping up and down, screaming, "Foreign devil!" It was my little friend from the Mud Flats. He had grown taller and his pigtail was gone but he was the same boy. I stepped over to him and leaned down.

"It's me," I said. "Look, it's me. Your American friend."

I could see in his eyes that he recognized me but not for a moment did he stop screaming.

I couldn't bear it. "I gave you oranges," I reminded him.

He spat on the ground. "Foreign devil!" he screamed.

I leaned closer. "Shut up!" I screamed back.

I turned and ran up the gangplank. As soon as I was on the boat, I gave a steel plate a hard kick.

My father was watching. "Who are you mad at?"

"The world," I answered. "The whole world."

With the steel plates up, the deck was dark and dismal and prisonlike. I had the sudden feeling that we

were all on an ark, waiting for a flood to begin, but this
ark wasn't big enough for two of a kind, so the men
would have to get off. Meanwhile we stood about in
little family clusters, hugging each other, giving advice,
saying good-bye. I called "Hello" to Nancy Little who
was standing close by with her family. Then the boat
gave a whistle and the men paraded single file down the
gangplank while the women and children stood behind
the steel plates, not even able to wave good-bye.

As soon as the boat had cleared the dock and was
headed downriver, the captain announced over the
loudspeaker that all passengers were to assemble in the
lounge. When we went in, the room was already
crowded—babies, children of all ages, and women of all
kinds: nuns, spike-heeled flappers, lame grandmothers,
fat mothers and thin ones, brave ones and sniffling ones.
Nancy, Margaret, Isobel, and I found each other and
sat down on the floor, waiting for the captain to speak,
which he was obviously going to do as soon as the room
had quieted down.

His speech was about safety. If we heard firing while
we were on deck, we were to throw ourselves immedi-
ately on the floor. The bullets, he said, would probably
just rattle against the plates and fall off, but there were
gaps between the plates and there was no telling how
heavy the firing might be. He explained all the emer-
gency procedures and told us where the life jackets and
lifeboats were. At night we were to pull the black cur-
tain that hung at our portholes so that the boat
wouldn't be easily seen. Finally, whenever we heard a
bell ring three times, we were to grab our life jackets
and hit the deck.

We were busy the rest of the day getting settled in
our cabins, but the next morning after breakfast Nancy

and I decided we should practice the safety measures. We talked Margaret and Isobel into being the enemy and hiding from us. Then as we strolled around the deck, they were to make rat-a-tat sounds and Nancy and I would fall to the deck. It was a good game and we played all day, improving our speed as we went along. When we got tired of plain falling, we tried different styles of falling. How would the nuns fall? we asked ourselves. And the flappers? We pretended that we were Mrs. Gale walking Nip and Tuck on their leashes, and although we let Mrs. Gale escape the bullets, we made sure that Nip and Tuck got it right in their hearts.

Back in the cabin at the end of the day, my mother told me that I was too old for that kind of game.

"I am?" I hadn't thought of myself as being too old for anything. I looked in the mirror. Of course I had grown taller, up to my mother's shoulders now and too big for any of my grandmother's petticoats. I studied my face to see if it had changed but all I could see was the same old face.

My mother looked over my shoulder. Then she licked her finger and reached around to smooth out my eyebrows. I was dumbfounded. I'd seen her smooth out her own eyebrows but surely it couldn't be time for me to pay attention to mine. Still, she kept looking at my reflection as if she were seeing someone who was not quite there yet.

"I certainly hope you don't have the Guttery eyes," she said. "It would be a shame if you had to wear glasses."

My mother didn't know that I was dying to wear glasses. All writers wore glasses and the sooner I got into them, I figured, the better. I moved away from the mirror because I knew what my mother was really thinking. Now she was hoping that I'd not only be good but that I'd turn pretty. I wanted to tell her to give up, but how could I? I was the only daughter she had.

The next day I told Nancy that I was bored by the falling-down game, so for the rest of the trip Nancy, Margaret, Isobel, and I spent most of our time in the lounge, playing snap and old maid. In any case, all that practice in falling down turned out to be a waste of time. No one had to fall down at all. The only bullets that hit the boat came at night when everyone was flat in bed anyway. I'd wake up with a jerk. Ping! Ping! Ping! And sometimes pingpingpingping. I'd burrow under my covers, wondering if a whole army was shooting at us or just a couple of soldiers on the riverbank. In the end it didn't matter. We got to Shanghai safely and on time.

My father had telegraphed Mrs. Hull about our arrival and she had sent someone to meet us and take care of our luggage. I worried about how much Andrea might have changed since learning the Charleston, and when she came to the door, my heart sank. There she was in silk stockings and there I was in woolen knee socks. There she was with her belt around her hips and there I was with my belt at the same old place around my waist. But as soon as she started to talk, I felt better.

"Guess what? Guess what?" She was full of news as always, but her mother hushed her.

"Later, Andrea," she said. "It will save. Let Jean and her mother take their coats off and settle down first."

My mother couldn't wait to settle down. "Any word from Arthur?" I knew she was hoping that there'd be a telegram, telling us that all was well and he'd see us for sure on the twentieth.

"No word from him. But there was a story in the paper yesterday." As soon as we were in the living room, Mrs. Hull handed my mother a clipping. I could tell it wasn't good news. Over my mother's shoulder I read that there had been rioting in Hankow. All foreign men had been staying overnight on boats where they would be safer.

My mother put the clipping down and looked out the window. "Well," she said, "I'm not going to America until Arthur gets here. No matter how long we have to wait."

I could see that Andrea was impatient. "But the paper doesn't say that people can't leave Hankow," she pointed out. "He better get here. Guess what?" She couldn't hold back her news any longer. "We have reservations on the *President Taft* too. We'll be going with you. David and Edward and Mother and I."

"*Really*? Oh, that's wonderful," I said. "Isn't that wonderful?"

Andrea grinned. "And how!"

"We'll just take for granted that Arthur will be here." Mrs. Hull spoke firmly to my mother. "We'll go right ahead and get ready. You may want to take up the hems on your skirts, Myrtle."

My mother seemed to cheer up as the talk turned to skirt lengths and I leaned over to Andrea. "I have to go to the bathroom," I whispered.

"Sure. Follow me."

I climbed the stairs behind Andrea's silk stockings. At the top she pointed out the rooms: her mother's room with its bath on one side; next to it the guest room (where my mother would be) and its bath; down the hall the boys' room.

I was keeping track. "Do they each have a bathroom?"

"No, they share. And they're not even here now. School is over for us and they're staying with my father in his apartment until we sail." She sighed. "We're having a hard time with David. He doesn't want to go to America."

"Does he have to? Can't he stay with your father?"

Andrea shook her head. "Both my mother and father think that would be bad for him. He'd just keep brooding and hoping. Maybe when he gets to a new country, he'll forget the adoption business."

I was interested in David Hull's troubles and I could see that Andrea wanted to talk about them, but right now I was more interested in the bathroom situation.

"You know," I said, "I'm kind of in a hurry."

"Sorry." Andrea took me into another bedroom. "We'll share my bedroom." She pointed to a door on the right. "My bathroom is there." Then she pointed to a door on the left. "That's yours there."

"My private bathroom?"

"Of course. I told you, didn't I?"

Well, that's all I wanted to know. I went in and shut the door. Right away, as if I'd been touched with a magic wand, I felt like a queen. I'd never dreamed that a bathroom could make so much difference in a person's life. Not only was it private, it was elegant. The basin and pot and tub were pale blue. The toilet paper too. (I'd always supposed all that stuff *had* to be white.) In one corner of the room was a dressing table with a blue-and-white-striped skirt flounced around it. I sat down on a chair in front of the table, picked up a comb, and ran it through my hair. I had never combed my hair sitting down before. Then I opened the door of the medicine cabinet and found little jars and tubes of face cream lined up inside. And a bottle of shampoo. And a big box of bath salts. I wondered if it would be all right for me to try out the bath salts. I flushed the toilet so Andrea would think I'd really had to go, then I went into the bedroom and asked about the bath salts.

"Sure you can use it. Help yourself to anything. I put it there just for you."

I was overwhelmed. "Do you always use bath salts?"

"And how!" Andrea was lying on the floor, just the way she used to, exercising her thighs.

"How come you say 'and how' so much?"

"It's the latest. They say it in the States all the time."

"Maybe when we get there, they'll be saying something different," I pointed out.

Andrea got up. "I can change. Want to see me do the split?" She took off her stockings so she wouldn't get a run and then glided to the floor as if her legs had been built to go in opposite directions.

She jumped up. "Now the back bend." Slowly she went over, all the way until the tips of her fingers touched the floor. Then a little more until her hands were down flat.

"I'm going on the stage," she announced.

She amazed me. She knew just how to get ready for life while all I seemed to do was to wait for life to happen.

That night I took a long, luxurious bath in deep, lilac-scented water. Afterward I sat down at the dressing table and on one side of my face I rubbed night cream that said "For oily skin." On the other side I rubbed cream that said "For dry skin." I'd never noticed what kind of skin I had so I figured this would

be a good test. Andrea called to me from the bedroom.

"Did you brush your hair?"

"*Now*? Why should I brush it now?"

"To keep it in good condition, you should brush fifty
strokes every night."

So I brushed. By the time I'd finished my beauty
work, it seemed a shame just to go to bed but that was
obviously all there was to do. I put on my flannel paja-
mas and Andrea put on her flowered nightgown and we
lay in the dark and talked and talked.

The next day after my mother and Mrs. Hull had
gone shopping, Andrea turned on the Victrola. I should
learn about popular music, she said. So I listened to
"Five Feet Two, Eyes of Blue" and "Gimme a Little
Kiss, Will Ya huh?" I didn't much care for the "Eyes of
Blue" song, but I agreed that "Gimme a Little Kiss"
had a nice snappy tune. Still, the song I liked best was
"I Scream, You Scream, We All Scream for Ice
Cream."

"You would," Andrea said.

"What do you mean—'I would'?"

"Well, it's not sophisticated or romantic. Your trouble is that you think America is just feeding your grandmother's chickens. There's a lot more to America than
that."

I supposed she was right. Still, I felt silly snapping my
fingers and singing "Five Feet Two" the way Andrea
did.

"Just remember," Andrea went on, "when you start
school in the States next fall, you'll be in eighth grade.
Nobody in the eighth grade is going to be singing 'Swa-
nee River.'"

She scared me.

"You don't still curtsy, I hope?"

"No."

"Well, thank goodness for that."

She made me feel so behind the times that when my mother came home and handed me a package of silk stockings, I went right upstairs and put them on, rolling the tops over round garters, the way Andrea did. Then I stretched out my legs to give them the once-over. They didn't look like my legs but I decided they weren't too bad. Still, I kept wondering: How on earth was I going to roller-skate in silk stockings?

The next day when my mother and Mrs. Hull came home from shopping, my mother seemed more light-hearted than she'd been for ages. "Well," she said, "I have a surprise."

She pulled off her hat and her hair was bobbed. I felt sick to my stomach. Andrea told her how stylish she looked, but I knew that she had ruined herself. She didn't look like my mother at all. I knew that my father would feel exactly the way I did. "What will Dad say?"

"Oh, he'll be mad at first," she said gaily, "but he'll get used to it."

When my father got mad, it was not a laughing matter. When his chin went hard, he was really trying to hold down the lid on a private volcano, but sometimes the lid blew. Sky-high.

"Don't you like it, Jean?" My mother was pirouetting around me.

"Well, you're pretty, no matter what you do." After all, she couldn't stick her hair back on, could she? When I looked at her, I'd just try to skip over her hair.

I had plenty of other things to think about. Mr. Hull was taking all the children to the moving pictures the next afternoon. Andrea was sorry that John Gilbert wasn't playing because she was in love with him, but this was next best, she said. Not a love movie, a scary one. *The Phantom of the Opera* with Lon Chaney. She said that a boy in the Shanghai American School had been so scared, he'd wet his pants. I could see that Andrea thought this movie was a real challenge, a test of how grown-up you were. I pretended to be excited too but secretly I was worried because I didn't know if I could pass the test. To make sure, I'd just close my eyes, I decided, if I felt any danger.

The way my mother and Mrs. Hull were tearing around—packing, shopping, sewing—you wouldn't have thought either one of them would have bothered to ask what we were going to see. But Mrs. Hull did, just as we were leaving. Andrea tried to get over the moment by shrugging and saying a loud good-bye, but David told.

"The Phantom of the Opera," he said.

Mrs. Hull grabbed Andrea's arm. "You are doing no such thing," she announced. She looked at Mr. Hull as if he'd taken leave of his senses. "You can't take children to that. *Rin-Tin-Tin* is playing across the street. Either the children go to that or they stay home."

"That's for babies!" Andrea cried. "Daddy promised us Lon Chaney."

But Mrs. Hull didn't care what Mr. Hull had promised and he didn't argue. After we'd left, Andrea tried to talk him into going to Lon Chaney anyway. "After all," she scoffed, "it's just a movie. How could a movie hurt anyone?"

But Mr. Hull took us to *Rin-Tin-Tin*. Secretly, of course, I was glad, because I knew I could keep my eyes open the whole time.

Actually, we should have gone to the movies the next day, the twentieth, and taken my mother to distract her. It was the day my father was due to arrive, and from the time she got up, my mother was beside herself. She would start a job, look at the clock, forget what she'd been doing, and go to another job. Every time the telephone rang, she jumped. Every time there was a knock at the door, she ran to it. It was never my father. In the evening she called up the boat company. No, they said, the boat from Hankow had not come in and they'd had no word.

The following day my mother paced. Every few hours she'd call up the boat company but there was still no news. I kept thinking of the pingpingpings on our boat; I kept worrying that my father didn't know how to fall down fast enough.

Andrea and I stayed downstairs late that night but at eleven o'clock, just as we were about to give up, there was a bang on the front door. My mother got there first.

And yes, it was my father, triumphant, laughing, happy, brimming with news of Narrow Squeaks. The boat, it seemed, had run aground in that shallow channel of the river that boats were always wary of. It had taken all this time to get clear. He told about the riots in Hankow and was reporting on what had happened to different friends when all at once I noticed that the line of my mother's mouth had gone tight and thin. My father had been here over half an hour, talking steadily about his news, and he hadn't even noticed her hair. After all, my mother had never had her hair cut in her life and of course she expected my father to be startled or shocked. But not even to notice! I was afraid that at any minute my mother might blow her own volcano, and I didn't want to be around, so I kissed them good night and went to bed.

I never did find out what went on between them but

the next morning everything seemed to be all right. I was the last one down for breakfast and right away I noticed how happy everyone was.

"The day after the day after tomorrow," Andrea announced.

Suddenly I felt as if a genie had clapped his hands and poof! my "ifs" had vanished. We all seemed to agree that nothing was going to stop us now. So we should celebrate, I thought. We should *do* something. We shouldn't just sit here eating oatmeal.

My father must have had the same feeling because all at once he slapped the table, tipped his chair back, and began singing "Pack Up Your Troubles in Your Old Kitbag and Smile, Smile, Smile." I looked at Andrea to see if she was turning up her nose at such an old-fashioned song, but no, she was grinning and singing along with everyone else.

I never knew grown-ups to stay excited for so long and I wondered when the spell would break. I knew, of course, that once we got on the ship, it would be hard for Andrea and David and Edward to say good-bye to their father, but no one was coming to say good-bye to me so I figured I could go on being happy indefinitely.

On the twenty-sixth, just before we went on the ship, my father sent my grandmother a cablegram: SAILING TODAY. I wanted him to add "Hooray," but every word cost money, he said, and besides she'd recognize the hooray even if it wasn't there. Certainly on board the *President Taft* the hooray feeling was all over the place. On deck the ship's band was playing "California, Here I Come," and people were dancing and singing and laughing. A steward was handing out rolls of paper streamers for passengers to throw over the railing as the ship sailed.

Although my mother, father, and I had spoken to Mr.
Hull when he'd first come on board with the boys, we'd
left him to visit alone with his children. I tried not to
look in their direction so I wouldn't spoil my hooray
feeling, but when the whistle blew for visitors to leave,
I went to Andrea and stood beside her. Together we
threw our streamers as the ship began to pull away
from the dock. Everyone threw. Roll after roll until the
distance from the ship to the dock was aflutter with
paper ribbons—red, yellow, blue, green. Flimsy things,
they looked as if they didn't want to let Shanghai go,
but of course as the ship moved farther away, they
broke, fell into the water, or simply hung bedraggled
over the ship's side. Andrea leaned over the railing,
waving to her father as long as she could see him. Then
suddenly she turned and ran—to her cabin, I supposed.

My mother, father, and Mrs. Hull went into the
lounge for tea. Edward went exploring, and I walked to
the back of the ship with David trailing behind me. It
seemed to me that once we were completely out of sight
of land, I would really feel homeward bound. But as I
looked at the Shanghai skyline and at the busy waterfront, I had the strange feeling that I wasn't moving
away at all. Instead the land was slowly moving away
and leaving me. Not just Shanghai but China itself.
It was as if I could see the whole country at once: all
the jogging rickshas, the pagodas, the squeaking wells,
the chestnut vendors, the water buffaloes, the bluebells,
the gray-coated soldiers, the bare-bottomed little boys.
And of course the muddy Yangtse with my own junk
looking at me with its wide eyes. I could even smell
China, and it was the smell of food cooking, of steam
rising from so many rice bowls it hung in a mist over
the land. But it was slipping away. No matter how hard

I squinted, it was fading from sight. I glanced at David, woebegone as always, but I knew he wasn't sad at leaving Mr. Hull or at leaving China. He was just feeling sorry for himself in the same old way.

Suddenly I was mad. "You make me sick, David Hull," I said. "Cry-babying over something in the past that you can't know a thing about. Don't you know your real past is right there? Yours and mine both." I pointed at China. "It's been under our noses the whole time and we've hardly noticed."

I didn't want to talk to David Hull, so I went down to the cabin to open Lin Nai-Nai's present. That would make me feel better, I thought. I took the red package out of my suitcase and tore off the tissue paper. Inside was a folded square of cloth that was obviously a piece of Lin Nai-Nai's embroidery. As I unfolded it, I drew in my breath. This was no iron-on pattern. This was Lin Nai-Nai's own design: a picture of a mountain, a thin black line climbing up to a scallop of clouds. In the center of the picture was a pool with bluebells and tiger lilies growing all around it. I started to cry—not just a flurry of sniffles but such huge sobs I had to throw myself on my bunk and bury my head in my pillow.

I heard my mother and father come into the cabin but I kept on crying. My mother leaned over me. "Whatever is the matter?" she asked.

I couldn't talk. I held up Lin Nai-Nai's embroidery for her to see.

"Of course," my mother said. "You miss Lin Nai-Nai."

That was true, but I was crying for more than that. For more than the memory of Kuling. For more than I could ever explain.

My mother put her arms around me. "You're just

tired," she said. "You'll feel better after a good night's sleep."

"That's right," my father agreed. "You'll be fine in the morning."

I wasn't tired. I knew I had good reasons for crying even if they were too mixed up to put into words.

Still, I did feel better the next morning. At eleven o'clock I was stretched out on a deck chair, my steamer rug over my legs. I was looking at the ocean and waiting for the steward to bring me a cup of beef tea.

6

It took twenty-eight days to go from Shanghai to San Francisco, and on that first morning I thought I'd be content to lie on my deck chair and stare at the ocean and drink beef tea the whole time. Not Andrea. She thought the ocean was one big waste. We should be watching the people, she said, and sizing them up as they went by. So we did. We found that mostly they fit into definite types. There were the Counters, for instance: fast-walking men, red-cheeked women, keeping score of how many times they walked around the deck, reveling in how fit they were. Then there were the Stylish Strollers, the Huffers and Puffers, the Lovebirds, leaning on each other, the Queasy Stomachs who clutched the railing and hoped for the best.

"You notice there's no one our age," Andrea said.

That was true. We had seen young people who were probably in their twenties, children who were Edward's age, and of course the majority who were our parents' age or older. But not one who might be in seventh or eighth grade or even high school.

Andrea jumped from her chair. "I'm going to explore."

Normally I would have gone with her but I hadn't had a chance yet to get my fill of the ocean. It was the same ocean as I'd had in Peitaiho and I looked and looked. I walked up to the top deck where I could see the whole circle of water around me. I was smack in the middle of no place, I thought. Not in China, not in America, not in the past, not in the future. In between everything. It was nice.

By the time I went back to my chair, Andrea had returned from her explorations.

"There really is no one our age on board," she reported.

"Well, we can play shuffleboard and deck tennis. There are lots of things we can do."

Andrea sighed. "I was hoping for some boys."

I knew that Andrea had begun to like boys. She said everyone at the Shanghai American School had a crush on someone else and when your love was requited— well, that was the cat's. What I couldn't understand was how someone could be in love with John Gilbert and a kid in knickers at the same time.

I suppose Andrea could see that I was trying to figure out the boy business. She gave me a curious look. "Just how do you picture your school in Washington, P.A.?" she asked.

Well, I knew exactly what it would be like, so I told her: I'd be an American in a class with nothing but Americans in it. When we fought the American Revolution, we'd all fight on the same side. When we sang "My country 'tis of thee," we'd yell our heads off. We'd all be the same. I would *belong*.

"There'll be boys in your class," Andrea pointed out.

"Naturally. I've seen boys before. So what?"

"Well, I think you're going to be surprised."

I didn't want to be surprised. For years I'd planned my first day at school in America.

"So how do you picture your school in Los Angeles, California?" I asked.

Andrea looked out at the ocean as if she expected to see her school sitting out there on the water. Then suddenly she shut her eyes and dropped her head in her hands. "Oh, Jean," she whispered, "I can't picture anything anymore. All I keep thinking about is my father. Alone in Shanghai."

This was as close as I'd ever seen Andrea come to crying. I put my hand on her shoulder. "I'm sorry," I said. Sorry! Such a puny word. You'd think the English language could give you something better. "I'm so sorry," I repeated.

Andrea dropped her hands and took a deep breath. "Well, let's play shuffleboard," she said.

From then on we played a lot of shuffleboard. Sometimes David joined us, but mostly he stayed in the ship's library, reading books about boys with real families. Edward kept busy in programs planned for children his age and the grown-ups made friends and talked their usual boring grown-up talk.

On the whole, Andrea and I had a good time on the *President Taft*. In the evenings we often watched movies. In the afternoons we made pigs of ourselves at tea where we had our pick of all kinds of dainty sandwiches, scones, macaroons, chocolate bonbons, and gooey tarts. Actually, I even liked going to bed on shipboard. I'd lie in my bunk and feel the ship's engines throbbing and know that even when I fell asleep I wouldn't be wasting time. I'd still be on the go, moving closer to America every minute.

Still, my "in-between" feeling stayed with me. One evening after supper I took Andrea to the top deck and told her about the feeling. Of course the "in-betweenness" was stronger than ever in the dark with the circle of water rippling below and the night sky above spilling over with stars. I had never seen so many stars. When I looked for a spot where I might stick an extra star if I had one, I couldn't find any space at all. No matter how small, an extra star would be out of place, I decided. The universe was one-hundred-percent perfect just as it was.

And then Andrea began to dance. She had slipped off her shoes and stockings and she was dancing what was obviously an "in-between" dance, leaping up toward the stars, sinking down toward the water, bending back toward China, reaching forward toward America, bending back again and again as if she could not tear herself away, yet each time dancing farther forward, swaying to and fro. Finally, her arms raised, she began twirling around, faster and faster, as if she were trying to outspin time itself. Scarcely breathing, I sat beside a smokestack and watched. She was making a poem and I was inside the poem with her. Under the stars, in the middle of the Pacific Ocean. I would never forget this night, I thought. Not if I lived to be one hundred.

Only when we came to the international date line did my "in-between" feeling disappear. This is the place, a kind of imaginary line in the ocean, where all ships going east add an extra day to that week and all ships going west drop a day. This is so you can keep up with the world turning and make time come out right. We had two Tuesdays in a row when we crossed the line and after that when it was "today" for me, I knew that Lin Nai-Nai was already in "tomorrow." I didn't like to think of Lin Nai-Nai so far ahead of me. It was as if we'd suddenly been tossed on different planets.

On the other hand, this was the first time in my life

that I was sharing the same day with my grand-mother.

Oh, Grandma, I thought, ready or not, here I come!

It was only a short time later that Edward saw a couple of rocks poking out of the water and yelled for us to come. The rocks could hardly be called land, but we knew they were the beginning of the Hawaiian Islands and we knew that the Hawaiian Islands were a territory belonging to the United States. Of course it wasn't the same as one of the forty-eight states; still, when we stepped off the *President Taft* in Honolulu (where we were to stay a couple of days before going on to San Francisco), we wondered if we could truthfully say we were stepping on American soil. I said no. Since the Hawaiian Islands didn't have a star in the flag, they couldn't be one-hundred-percent American, and I wasn't going to consider myself on American soil until I had put my feet flat down on the state of California.

We had a week to wait. The morning we were due to arrive in San Francisco, all the passengers came on deck early, but I was the first. I skipped breakfast and went to the very front of the ship where the railing comes to a point. That morning I would be the "eyes" of the *President Taft,* searching the horizon for the first speck of land. My private ceremony of greeting, however, would not come until we were closer, until we were sailing through the Golden Gate. For years I had heard about the Golden Gate, a narrow stretch of water connecting the Pacific Ocean to San Francisco Bay. And for years I had planned my entrance.

Dressed in my navy skirt, white blouse, and silk stockings, I felt every bit as neat as Columbus or Balboa and every bit as heroic when I finally spotted America in the distance. The decks had filled with passengers by

now, and as I watched the land come closer, I had to tell myself over and over that I was HERE. At last.

Then the ship entered the narrow stretch of the Golden Gate and I could see American hills on my left and American houses on my right, and I took a deep breath of American air.

" 'Breathes there the man, with soul so dead,' " I cried,

" 'Who never to himself hath said,

This is my own, my native land!' "

I forgot that there were people behind and around me until I heard a few snickers and a scattering of claps, but I didn't care. I wasn't reciting for anyone's benefit but my own.

Next for my first steps on American soil, but when the time came, I forgot all about them. As soon as we were on the dock, we were jostled from line to line. Believe it or not, after crossing thousands of miles of ocean to get here, we had to prove that it was O.K. for us to come into the U.S.A. We had to show that we were honest-to-goodness citizens and not spies. We had to open our baggage and let inspectors see that we weren't smuggling in opium or anything else illegal. We even had to prove that we were germ-free, that we didn't have smallpox or any dire disease that would infect the country. After we had finally passed the tests, I expected to feel one-hundred-percent American. Instead, stepping from the dock into the city of San Francisco, I felt dizzy and unreal, as if I were a made-up character in a book I had read too many times to believe it wasn't still a book. As we walked the Hulls to the car that their Aunt Kay had driven up from Los Angeles, I told Andrea about my crazy feeling.

"I'm kind of funny in the head," I said. "As if I'm not really me. As if this isn't really happening."

"Me too," Andrea agreed. "I guess our brains haven't caught up to us yet. But my brains better get going. Guess what?"

"What?"

"Aunt Kay says our house in Los Angeles is not far from Hollywood."

Then suddenly the scene speeded up and the Hulls were in the car, ready to leave for Los Angeles, while I was still stuck in a book without having said any of the things I wanted to. I ran after the car as it started.

"Give my love to John Gilbert," I yelled to Andrea.

She stuck her head out the window. "And how!" she yelled back.

My mother, father, and I were going to stay in a hotel overnight and start across the continent the next morning, May 24, in our new Dodge. The first thing we did now was to go to a drugstore where my father ordered three ice-cream sodas. "As tall as you can make them," he said. "We have to make up for lost time."

My first American soda was chocolate and it was a whopper. While we sucked away on our straws, my father read to us from the latest newspaper. The big story was about America's new hero, an aviator named Charles Lindbergh who had just made the first solo flight across the Atlantic Ocean. Of course I admired him for having done such a brave and scary thing, but I bet he wasn't any more surprised to have made it across one ocean than I was to have finally made it across another. I looked at his picture. His goggles were pushed back on his helmet and he was grinning. He had it all over John Gilbert, I decided. I might even consider having a crush on him—that is, if and when I ever felt the urge. Right now I was coming to the bottom of my soda and I was trying to slurp up the last drops when my mother told me to quit; I was making too much noise.

The rest of the afternoon we spent sight-seeing, riding up and down seesaw hills in cable cars, walking in and out of American stores. Every once in a while I found myself smiling at total strangers because I knew that if I were to speak to them in English, they'd answer in English. We were all Americans. Yet I still felt as if I were telling myself a story. America didn't become completely real for me until the next day after we'd left San Francisco and were out in the country.

My father had told my mother and me that since he wasn't used to our new car or to American highways, we should be quiet and let him concentrate. My mother concentrated too. Sitting in the front seat, she flinched every time she saw another car, a crossroad, a stray dog, but she never said a word. I paid no attention to the road. I just kept looking out the window until all at once there on my right was a white picket fence and a meadow, fresh and green as if it had just this minute been created. Two black-and-white cows were grazing slowly over the grass as if they had all the time in the world, as if they knew that no matter how much they ate, there'd always be more, as if in their quiet munching way they understood that they had nothing, nothing whatsoever to worry about. I poked my mother, pointed, and whispered, "Cows." I had never seen cows in China but it was not the cows themselves that impressed me. It was the whole scene. The perfect greenness. The washed-clean look. The peacefulness. Oh, *now*! I thought. Now I was in America. Every last inch of me.

By the second day my father acted as if he'd been

driving the car all his life. He not only talked, he sang, and if he felt like hitching up his trousers, he just took his hands off the wheel and hitched. But as my father relaxed, my mother became more tense. "Arthur," she finally said, "you are going forty-five."

My father laughed. "Well, we're headed for the stable, Myrtle. You never heard of a horse that dawdled on its way home, did you?"

My mother's lips went tight and thin. "The whole point of driving across the continent," she said, "was so we could see the country."

"Well, it's all there." My father swept his hand from one side of the car to the other. "All you have to do is to take your eyes off the road and look." He honked his horn at the car in front of him and swung around it.

At the end of the day, after we were settled in an overnight cabin, my father took a new notebook from his pocket. I watched as he wrote: "May 24. 260 miles." Just as I'd suspected, my father was out to break records. I bet that before long we'd be making 300 miles or more a day. I bet we'd be in Washington, P.A., long before July.

The trouble with record breaking is that it can lead to Narrow Squeaks, and while we were still in California we had our first one. Driving along a back road that my father had figured out was a shortcut, we came to a bridge with a barrier across it and a sign in front: THIS BRIDGE CONDEMNED. DO NOT PASS. There was no other road marked DETOUR, so obviously the only thing to do was to turn around and go back about five miles to the last town and take the regular highway. My father stopped the car. "You'd think they'd warn you in advance," he muttered. He slammed the door, jumped over the barrier, and walked onto the bridge. Then he climbed down the riverbank and looked up at the bridge from below. When he came back up the bank, he pushed the barrier aside, got in the car, and started it up. "We can make it," he said.

It hadn't occurred to me that he'd try to drive across. My mother put her hand on his arm. "Please, Arthur," she begged, but I didn't bother with any "pleases." If he wanted to kill himself, he didn't have to kill Mother and me too. "Let Mother and me walk across," I shouted. "Let us out. Let us OUT."

My father had already revved up the motor. "A car can have only one driver," he snapped. "I'm it." He backed up so he could get a flying start and then we whooped across the bridge, our wheels clattering across the loose boards, space gaping below. Well, we did reach the other side and when I looked back, I saw that the bridge was still there.

"You see?" my father crowed. "You see how much time we saved?"

All I could see was that we'd risked our lives because he was so pigheaded. Right then I hated my father. I felt rotten hating someone I really loved but I couldn't help it. I knew the loving would come back but I had to wait several hours.

There were days, however, particularly across the long, flat stretches of Texas, when nothing out-of-the-way happened. We just drove on and on, and although my father reported at the end of the day that we'd gone 350 miles, the scenery was the same at the end as at the beginning, so it didn't feel as if we'd moved at all. Other times we ran into storms or into road construction and we were lucky if we made 200 miles. But the best day of the whole trip, at least as far as my mother and I were concerned, was the day that we had a flat tire in the Ozark Mountains. The spare tire and jack were buried in the trunk under all our luggage, so everything had to be taken out before my father could even begin work on the tire. There was no point in offering to help because my father had a system for loading and unloading which only he understood, so my mother and I set off up the mountainside, looking for wild flowers.

"Watch out for snakes," my mother said, but her voice was so happy, I knew she wasn't thinking about snakes.

As soon as I stepped out of the car, I fell in love with the day. With the sky—fresh, blotting-paper blue. With the mountains, warm and piney and polka-dotted with flowers we would never have seen from the window of a car. We decided to pick one of each kind and press them in my gray geography book which I had in the car. My mother held out her skirt, making a hollow out of it, while I dropped in the flowers and she named them: forget-me-not, wintergreen, pink, wild rose. When we didn't know the name, I'd make one up: pagoda plant, wild confetti, French knot. My mother's skirt was atumble with color when we suddenly realized how far we'd walked. Holding her skirt high, my mother led the way back, running and laughing. We arrived at the car, out of breath, just as my father was loading the last of the luggage into the trunk. He glared at us, his face streaming with perspiration. "I don't have a dry stitch on me," he said, as if it were our fault that he sweat so much. Then he looked at the flowers in Mother's skirt and his face softened. He took out his handkerchief and wiped his face and neck and finally he smiled. "I guess I picked a good place to have a flat tire, didn't I?" he said.

The farther we went, the better mileage we made, so that by the middle of June we were almost to the West Virginia state line. My father said we'd get to Washington, P.A., the day after the next, sometime in the afternoon. He called my grandmother on the phone, grinning because he knew how surprised she'd be. I stood close so I could hear her voice.

"Mother?" he said when she answered. "How about stirring up a batch of flannel cakes?"

"Arthur!" (She sounded just the way I knew she would.) "Well, land's sakes, Arthur, where are you?"

"About ready to cross into West Virginia."

My grandmother was so excited that her words fell over each other as she tried to relay the news to my grandfather and Aunt Margaret and talk over the phone at the same time.

The next day it poured rain and although that didn't slow us down, my mother started worrying. Shirls Avenue, my grandparents' street, apparently turned into a dirt road just before plunging down a steep hill to their house and farm. In wet weather the road became one big sea of mud which, according to my mother, would be "worth your life to drive through."

"If it looks bad," my mother suggested, "we can park at the top of the hill and walk down in our galoshes."

My father sighed. "Myrtle," he said, "we've driven across the Mohave Desert. We've been through thick and thin for over three thousand miles and here you are worrying about Shirls Avenue."

The next day the sun was out, but when we came to Shirls Avenue, I could see that the sun hadn't done a thing to dry up the hill. My father put the car into low, my mother closed her eyes, and down we went, sloshing up to our hubcaps, careening from one rut to another, while my father kept one hand down hard on the horn to announce our arrival.

By the time we were at the bottom of the hill and had parked beside the house, my grandmother, my grandfather, and Aunt Margaret were all outside, looking exactly the way they had in the calendar picture. I ran right into my grandmother's arms as if I'd been doing this every day.

"Welcome home! Oh, welcome home!" my grandmother cried.

I hadn't known it but this was exactly what I'd wanted her to say. I needed to hear it said out loud. I was home.

7

WHEN AUNT MARGARET TOOK ME TO THE BACK
of the house to show me around, I found everything so
familiar I didn't need to be told what was what.
"Here's the grape arbor," I said, and I ran through the
long archway that led from the back door to what was
once the stable but was now a garage for my grandfather's truck.

"Oh, and there's the pump!"

"We have running water now," Aunt Margaret
explained, "so we don't use the pump much."

"But I can pump if I want to, can't I?"

"Sure you can."

Running up the hill on one side of the house was the
cornfield. Running down the hill on the other side was
the vegetable garden, the rhubarb plot, the dahlia beds.
At the bottom of the hill was my grandfather's greenhouse.

"Where are the chickens?" I asked.

"Around the corner."

As we went to the other side of the house, a brown-
and-white-speckled rooster came strutting to meet us.

"That's Josh," Aunt Margaret said. "He's such a seri-
ous-minded rooster, he can't stand to hear anyone
laugh. He ruffles up his feathers and cusses his head
off."

I squatted down and tried to force a laugh. "Ha ha-
ha ha."

"No," Aunt Margaret said, "he knows you're just pretending."

Not far behind Josh was the chicken house with a big fenced-in yard around it. I ran over and looked at the hens, teetering like plump little ladies on spike heels.

"What are their names?" I asked.

"They don't have names."

"How come?"

"We don't want to become too fond of them."

I'd never heard anything so silly. If I was going to feed them, I ought to know their names. "Why not?" I asked.

"Well, Jean," Aunt Margaret explained, "you know that this is a farm. In the end we eat every one of those chickens."

I felt dumb not to have known. I decided that when I fed the chickens, I'd try not to even look them in the eye.

As we went inside, Aunt Margaret pointed to a pair of roller skates on the back porch. "I dug those out of the attic," she said. "I thought you'd like them." She looked at my legs. "But you can't roller-skate in silk stockings."

"That's O.K.," I grinned. "I have socks."

Of course I wanted to try the roller skates right away but my mother's family was due to arrive for a welcome-home party and all of us had to get dressed up.

"Are we going to have flannel cakes?" I asked.

Aunt Margaret laughed. "That was just a joke. We're going to have potato salad and smearcase and cold chicken and apple pie and lots of other good things. We've been cooking ever since your father called."

My mother's family arrived all at once: Aunt Blanche, Aunt Etta, Aunt Mary L., Aunt Sarah and

Uncle Welsh, Uncle George and Aunt Edith, and my four cousins—Elizabeth and Jane who were much older and Katherine and Charlotte who were about three years younger. There were a couple of extra girls, but I couldn't figure out where they fit in. The family parked their cars at the top of the hill, stopped to pull on galoshes, and then picked their way down the grassy side of the road which was fairly dry. When my mother saw them, she ran up the hill, her arms out, and I watched one of her sisters run ahead of the others, her arms out too. I knew it must be Aunt Blanche. They stood beside the road, hugging, stepping back to make sure who they were, then hugging again. When the whole family got to the bottom of the hill where my father and I were waiting, everyone began crying and laughing and kissing and hugging at the same time. I never saw such carrying-on. Not just one kiss apiece, but kiss after kiss while I was still trying to figure out which aunt was which.

My youngest cousin, Charlotte, who was watching all this, suggested that we clear out until the excitement had died down. Those two other girls tagged along as we went to the back of the house where we all sat down on the platform surrounding the pump.

"I can't stand all that kissing business," Charlotte said. "Can you?"

"No," I agreed. "They wouldn't even let me get my breath."

"Let's make a pact," she suggested. "I'll never kiss you if you promise never to kiss me."

We shook on it. But I still wondered about those other two girls, so I whispered to Charlotte, asking if they were related. She said no, they were neighbor kids who had begged to come along because they wanted to see the girl from China. "This is Ruth and this is Marie," she said, but I could tell she wished they were someplace else.

Up to this time Ruth and Marie had just stared at me, but now Ruth nudged Marie and whispered, "You ask."

Marie giggled. "We want to know if you ate rats in China and what they tasted like."

"And if you ate their *tails* too," Ruth added.

Rats! "No one in China eats rats," I said stiffly.

"Oh, you don't need to pretend." Ruth was smuggling her laughter behind her hands. "Everyone knows that people in China eat queer things. Snakes, birds' nests . . ."

"They do not."

The girls were looking at me as if I were some kind of a freak in a circus. As if maybe I had two heads.

"Did you use sticks to eat with?" Marie asked.

"Chopsticks, you mean. Sometimes. Of course."

Both girls lay back on the platform, shrieking with laughter. Josh came tearing around the house, scolding, ruffling his feathers, and I didn't blame him. He wasn't any madder than I was.

"Quit it," I told the girls. "You're upsetting the rooster."

This only set them off again. When they finally got control of themselves, they asked if I could speak Chinese and I said yes, I certainly could.

I turned to Marie and said in Chinese, "Your mother is a big turtle." ("Nide muchin shr ega da wukwei.") Then I looked at Ruth and told her that her mother was a turtle too. I knew that in English it wouldn't sound so bad but in China this was an insult.

The girls were rolling all over the platform in spasms

of laughter while Josh croaked and flapped. "Oh, it sounds so funny, say it again," Ruth begged.

So I did. And I added that they were worthless daughters of baboons and they should never have been born.

"What does it mean?" they asked. "Tell us what it means."

"You wouldn't understand," I said coldly. "Come on, Charlotte, let's go back to the party."

That night after everyone had left, I told my mother and father about the crazy questions Ruth and Marie had asked.

"Well, Jean," my father said, "some people in Washington don't know any better. China seems so far away they imagine strange things."

I told myself that only little kids like Ruth and Marie could be so ignorant. Eighth graders would surely know better.

But for a while I didn't worry about eighth grade. I spent the summer doing the things I had dreamed about. Charlotte and I roller-skated, and although it didn't take me long to learn, my knees were skinned most of the time. I didn't care. I was proud of every one of my scabs; they showed that I was having a good time. And there were so many ways to have a good time—so many flavors of ice cream to try, so many treasures to choose at the five-and-ten, so many trees to climb, so many books to borrow from the library, so many relatives willing to stop for a game of dominoes or checkers. My grandfather and I played horseshoes, and although I never beat him, he said I was every bit as good as my father had been at my age.

And I helped my grandmother. Sometimes I spent the whole day working beside her: shelling peas, kneading bread dough, turning the handle of the wringer after she'd washed clothes, feeding the chickens, sweeping the porch. In China I'd had nothing to do with the work of the house. It just went on automatically around me as if it could have been anyone's house, but now suddenly I was a part of what went on. I had a place. For instance. My grandmother might ask me if we had enough sugar in the house or should she get some, and likely as not, I would know.

"The sugar bin is getting low," I would say. "Maybe you should buy another bag."

Then my grandmother would add "sugar" to her shopping list and she'd say she didn't know how she'd ever got along without me. I loved to hear her say that even though I knew she'd done fine without me. But I did have a lot of new accomplishments. I wrote to Lin Nai-Nai and described them to her. I could even do coolie work, I told her. I could mow grass. I could mop floors.

Still, I thought about school. I'd always supposed I knew exactly what an American school would be like, but as the time came near, I wasn't sure. Suppose I didn't fit in? Suppose I wasn't the same as everyone else, after all? Suppose I turned out to be another Vera Sebastian? Suppose eighth graders thought I was a rat eater?

I couldn't forget the first Sunday I'd gone to church in Washington. The other kids in church had poked each other when I'd walked in. "There's the girl from China." I knew by their faces that's what they were thinking. The woman who sat behind me had made no bones about it. I overheard her whispering to her husband. "You can tell she wasn't born in this country," she said. How could she tell? I wondered. If just looking at me made people stare, what would happen when they heard me talk? Suppose I said something silly? I remembered the rainy afternoon at my grandmother's when we were all sitting around reading and I had come to a word that I didn't know.

"What's a silo?" I asked.

The way everyone looked up so surprised, it was as if they were saying, "How on earth did she live this long without knowing what a silo is?" Of course when my father explained, I realized I'd seen silos all over the country; I just hadn't known what they were called. But suppose I had asked that question in school!

I kept pestering Aunt Margaret to tell me if there was anything about eighth grade that I should know and didn't.

"It doesn't matter," she would say. "Not everyone in eighth grade is going to know exactly the same things."

Aunt Margaret had a new beau and I suspected that she wasn't giving my eighth-grade problems enough serious thought, but one day she did ask me if I knew the Pledge of Allegiance.

"What Pledge of Allegiance?"

So she explained that every morning we'd start off by pledging allegiance to the flag and she taught me how to say it, my hand over my heart. After that, I practiced every day while I was feeding the chickens. I'd clap my hand over my heart and tell them about "one nation indivisible." It gave me courage. Surely if the whole class felt strongly about the American flag, I'd fit in all right.

My mother and father would be away when school started. Toward the end of the summer they had begun to give lectures in order to raise money for the

Y.M.C.A. and now they were going to Canada for two weeks. Before they left, my mother called the school principal to notify him that I'd be entering eighth grade. She gave Aunt Margaret money to buy me a new dress for school. When she kissed me good-bye, she smoothed out my eyebrows.

"Be good," she whispered.

I stiffened. I wondered if she'd ever forget goodness. Probably the last thing she'd say to me before I walked up the aisle to be married was "Be good."

The next day Aunt Margaret took me to Caldwell's store on Main Street and bought me a red-and-black-plaid gingham dress with a white collar and narrow black patent leather belt that went around my hips. She took me to a beauty parlor and I had my hair shingled.

When I got home, I tried on my dress. "How do I look?" I asked my grandmother.

"As if you'd just stepped out of a bandbox."

I wasn't sure that was the look I was aiming for. "But do I look like a regular eighth grader?"

"As regular as they come," she assured me.

The day before school started, I laid out my new dress and stockings and shoes so I'd be ready. I put aside the loose-leaf notebook Aunt Margaret had given me. I pledged allegiance to the chickens and then I sat down on the back steps next to my grandmother who was shelling peas. I reached into her lap, took a bunch of peas, and began shelling into the pan.

"I wish my name were Marjorie," I said. "I'd feel better starting to school with the name Marjorie."

My grandmother split a pea pod with her thumbnail and sent the peas plummeting into the pan.

"Do you like the name Marjorie?" I asked.

"Not much. It sounds common."

"But that's the idea!" I said. "It would make me fit in with everyone else."

"I thought you were going to be a writer."

"I am."

"Well, my stars! Writers do more than just fit in. Sometimes they don't fit in at all." My grandmother quit shelling and looked straight at me. "You know why I like the name *Jean*?" she asked.

"Why?"

"It's short and to the point; it doesn't fool around. Like my name—Isa. They're both good, strong Scottish names. Spunky."

I'd never known my name was Scottish. I surely had never thought of it as strong.

"Grandma," I said, "do you worry about whether I'm good or not?"

My grandmother threw back her head and hooted. "Never. It hasn't crossed my mind." She gave my knee a slap. "I love you just the way you are."

I leaned against her, wanting to say "thank you" but thinking that this wasn't the kind of thing that you said "thank you" for.

The next morning my grandmother and grandfather watched me start up Shirls Avenue in my new outfit, my notebook under my arm.

"Good luck!" they called. I held up my hand with my fingers crossed.

The school was about four blocks away—a big, red-brick, square building that took care of all grades, kindergarten through the eighth. So, of course, there were all ages milling about, but I looked for the older ones. When I'd spotted some—separate groups of girls and boys laughing and talking—I decided that I didn't look any different, so I went into the building, asked in the office where the eighth grade was, and went upstairs to the first room on the right.

Others were going into the room, and when I saw that they seemed to sit wherever they wanted, I picked a desk about halfway up the row next to the window. I slipped my notebook into the open slot for books and then looked at the teacher who was standing, her back to us, writing on the blackboard. She had a thick, straight-up, corseted figure and gray hair that had been marcelled into such stiff, even waves I wondered if she dared put her head down on a pillow at night.

"My name is Miss Crofts," she had written.

She didn't smile or say "Good Morning" or "Welcome to eighth grade" or "Did you have a nice summer?" She just looked at the clock on the wall and when it was exactly nine o'clock, she tinkled a bell that was like the one my mother used to call the servants.

"The class will come to order," she said. "I will call the roll." As she sat down and opened the attendance book, she raised her right index finger to her head and very carefully she scratched so she wouldn't disturb the waves. Then she began the roll:

Margaret Bride (*Here*). Donald Burch (*Here*), Andrew Carr (*Present*). Betty Donahue (*Here*).

I knew the G's would be coming pretty soon.

John Goodman (*Here*), Jean Guttery.

Here, I said. Miss Crofts looked up from her book. "Jean Guttery is new to our school," she said. "She has come all the way from China where she lived beside the Yangs-Ta-Zee River. Isn't that right, Jean?"

"It's pronounced *Yang-see,*" I corrected. "There are just two syllables."

Miss Crofts looked at me coldly. "In America," she said, "we say Yangs-Ta-Zee."

I wanted to suggest that we look it up in the dictionary, but Miss Crofts was going right on through the roll. She didn't care about being correct or about the Yangtse River or about me and how I felt.

Miss Crofts, I said to myself, your mother is a turtle. A big fat turtle.

I was working myself up, madder by the minute, when I heard Andrew Carr, the boy behind me, shifting his feet on the floor. I guess he must have hunched across his desk, because all at once I heard him whisper over my shoulder:

"Chink, Chink Chinaman
Sitting on a fence,
Trying to make a dollar
Out of fifteen cents."

I forgot all about where I was. I jumped to my feet, whirled around, and spoke out loud as if there were no Miss Crofts, as if I'd never been in a classroom before, as if I knew nothing about classroom behavior.

"You don't call them Chinamen or Chinks," I cried. "You call them *Chinese*. Even in America you call them *Chinese*."

The class fell absolutely silent, all eyes on me, and for the first time I really looked at Andrew Carr. I think I had expected another Ian Forbes, but he was just a freckle-faced kid who had turned beet-red. He was slouched down in his seat as if he wished he could disappear.

Miss Crofts stood up. "Will someone please explain to me what all this is about?"

The girl beside me spoke up. "Andrew called Jean a Chinaman."

"Well, you don't need to get exercised, Jean," she said. "We all know that you are American."

"But that's not the *point!*" Before I could explain

that it was an insult to call Chinese people *Chinamen,* Miss Crofts had tapped her desk with a ruler.

"That will be enough," she said. "All eyes front." Obediently the students stopped staring and turned their attention to Miss Crofts. All but one boy across the room. He caught my eye, grinned, and put his thumb up, the way my father did when he thought I'd done well. I couldn't help it; I grinned back. He looked nice, I thought.

"We will stand now and pledge allegiance," Miss Crofts announced. Even though I still felt shaky, I leaped to attention. I wasn't going to let anything spoil my first official pledge. As I placed my hand on my heart, I glanced around. The girl next to me had her hand on her stomach.

"I pledge allegiance to the flag of the United States of America." The class mumbled, but maybe that was because of the flag. It was the saddest-looking flag I'd ever seen, standing in the corner, its stars and stripes drooping down as if they had never known a proud moment. So as I pledged, I pictured the American flag on the Bund, waving as if it were telling the world that America was the land of the free and the home of the brave. Maybe I made my pledge too loud, because when I sat down, the boy across the room raised his thumb again. I hoped he wasn't making fun of me but he seemed friendly so I smiled back.

When I looked at Miss Crofts, she had her finger in her hair and she was daintily working her way through another wave.

After the commotion I had already made in the class, I decided to be as meek as I possibly could the rest of the morning. Since this was the first day at school, we would be dismissed at noon, and surely things would improve by then.

Miss Crofts put a bunch of history books on the first desk of each row so they could be passed back, student to student. I was glad to see that we'd be studying the history of Pennsylvania. Since both my mother's and father's families had helped to settle Washington County, I was interested to know how they and other pioneers had fared. Opening the book to the first chapter, "From Forest to Farmland," I skimmed through the pages but I couldn't find any mention of people at all. There was talk about dates and square miles and cultivation and population growth and immigration and the Western movement, but it was as if the forests had lain down and given way to farmland without anyone being brave or scared or tired or sad, without babies being born, without people dying. Well, I thought, maybe that would come later.

After history, we had grammar and mathematics, but the most interesting thing that I learned all morning was that the boy across the room was named Donald Burch. He had sandy-colored hair combed straight back and he wore a sky-blue shirt.

The last class was penmanship. I perked up because I knew I was not only good at penmanship, but I enjoyed making my words run across a page, round and neat and happy-looking. At the British School we had always printed, so I had learned to make my letters stand up straight and even, and when I began to connect up my letters for handwriting, I kept that proud, straight-up look.

I took the penmanship workbooks from the girl in front of me, kept my copy, and passed the rest to Andrew Carr. The workbook was called *The Palmer Method,* but the title was not printed; it was handwritten in big, oversized, sober-looking letters, slanting to the right. If you pulled one letter out of a word, I thought, the rest would topple over like a row of dominoes.

"Jean," Miss Crofts said after the workbooks had been distributed, "I expect you have not been exposed to the Palmer method of penmanship. The rest of the class will work on Exercise One, but I want you to come up to my desk while I explain the principle of Palmer penmanship."

Slowly I dragged myself to the front of the room and sat down in the chair that Miss Crofts had pulled up beside her own.

"You see," Miss Crofts said, "in the Palmer method you really write with the underside of your forearm. The fleshy part." She pointed to her own forearm which was quite fleshy and then she put it down on the desk. "You hold your fingers and wrist stiff. All the movement comes from your arm. You begin by rotating the flesh on your arm so that your pen will form slanting circles." She filled a line on the paper with falling-down circles. "When you have mastered the circles," she said, "your arm will be ready for the letters."

As Miss Crofts looked at me to see if I understood, she made a quick dive with her index finger into her waves.

I folded my hands in my lap. "I have very good penmanship," I said. "No one has trouble reading it. I really do not care to change my style."

Miss Crofts pushed a pen and a pad of paper in front of me. "The Palmer method has been proved to be the most efficient system." She had so many years of teaching behind her I could see she wasn't going to fool around. "Just put your arm on the desk, Jean," she said, "and try some circles."

"I don't think I have enough flesh on the underside of my arm," I whispered. "I'm too skinny."

Miss Crofts reached over, picked up my arm, put it on the desk, and pushed a pen in my hand. "Just roll your arm around but keep your fingers stiff. Let your arm do the work."

Sitting in front of the room with everyone peeking up at me from their workbooks, I was afraid I was going to cry. How could I stand to let my letters lean over as if they were too tired to say what they wanted straight out? How could I ever write a poem if I couldn't let the words come out through my fingers and feel their shape? I glanced at Donald Burch who, like everyone else, must have seen how miserable I was. He tapped his forehead to show how crazy Miss Crofts was. Then he shrugged as if he were saying, "What can you do with a nitwit like that?"

I moved my arm halfheartedly and produced a string of sick-looking circles.

"I think you have the idea," Miss Crofts said. "You may go to your seat and practice."

So I went to my seat but I didn't make a single circle unless I saw Miss Crofts watching me. I just hunched over my workbook, promising myself that I would never use the Palmer method outside the classroom. Never. I wouldn't even try hard in the classroom and if I flunked penmanship, so what? I kept looking at the clock, waiting and waiting for the big hand to crawl up and meet the little hand at *Twelve*. When it finally did, Miss Crofts tinkled her bell.

"Class—attention!" she ordered. We all stood up. "First row, march!" Row by row we marched single file out the door, down the stairs, and into the free world where the sun was shining.

Donald Burch was standing on the sidewalk and as I came up, he fell into step beside me.

"She's a real bird, isn't she?" he said.

"You said it!" I glanced up at him. He was two inches taller than I was. "Where do you suppose she dug up the Palmer method?"

"It's not just here," Donald said. "It's all over. Every school in the country uses it."

I stopped in my tracks. "All over *America*?"

"Yep."

I had a sudden picture of schools in every one of the forty-eight states grinding out millions and millions of sheets of paper covered with leaning letters exactly alike. "But what about liberty for all?" I cried. "Why do they want to make us copycats?"

Donald shrugged. "Search me. Grown-ups don't write all the same. Dumb, isn't it?"

As we walked on together, I began to feel better, knowing that Donald felt the same way as I did. Besides, I'd had a good look at him now. When he grew up, he might look a little like Charles Lindbergh, I decided, especially if he wore goggles.

"I guess you never had anyone as bad as Miss Crofts in your school in China, did you?" he asked.

"Well, I had one teacher who was pretty bad, but I think Miss Crofts has her beat."

"Did you like living in China?" Donald asked.

"Yes." (*Oh, please, I prayed, please don't let him ask me if I ate rats.*)

"I bet it was nice. But you know something?"

"What?"

"I'm sure glad you came back to America." He squinted at the sky as if he were trying to figure out the weather. "How about you? Are you glad you came back?"

"And how!" I didn't say it; I breathed it. At the same time I began mentally composing a letter to Andrea.

Dear Andrea: I started school today and there's this boy in my class. Donald Burch. He is the CAT'S!

We had come to Shirls Avenue now. I pointed down the hill. "That's where I live," I said. "That's my grandparents' farm down there. Where do you live?"

Donald pointed over his shoulder. "Back there a few blocks."

He had come out of his way.

"O.K. if I walk with you again tomorrow?" he asked.

I'm sure I said it would be O.K., although all I remember as I ran down the hill was thinking: Oh, I'm in love, I'm in love, and I think it's requited!

When I came to the bottom of the hill, I called out that I was home and my grandmother yoo-hooed from the vegetable garden. I found her among the carrots, standing up in her long white, starched apron, waiting for me, smiling.

"My, you look happy," she said.

I grinned. "I made a friend," I explained.

"Good! That's the best thing that could happen. And how about school?"

I came down to earth with a thump. There was no way I could look happy with a question like that to answer. I just shook my head.

"So it wasn't one-hundred-percent," my grandmother said. "Few things are."

"It was a flop."

"Who's your teacher?"

"Miss Crofts."

"My stars!" My grandmother put her hands on her hips. "Don't tell me she's still hanging around? Why, Margaret had her."

"She's still hanging around," I said.

My grandmother's face took on a sly, comical look. She put her index finger to her head and scratched carefully. "Still scratching, is she?"

Her imitation was so perfect, I burst out laughing.

"Still scratching," I said.

My grandmother and I laughed together and once started, we couldn't seem to stop. We'd let up for a second, then look at each other, and one of us would scratch, and we'd break out again. In fact, it felt so good to laugh, I didn't want to stop.

"She must have cooties," I gasped.

"She ought to have her head examined." And off we went again!

By this time Josh, who had joined us at the first explosion, was throwing himself about in an outrage, but I couldn't let a rooster spoil the fun. Coming to the surface from my last spasm, I told my grandmother about the Palmer method.

"We're supposed to write with the underside of our arms." I showed her where. "We can't move our fingers or our wrists."

At first my grandmother couldn't believe me, but as I went on about the workbooks and circles, she dissolved into another round of laughter. She turned toward the greenhouse where my grandfather was working. "Will," she called. "Oh, Will! Come and hear this!"

Well, I decided, the only thing a person could do about the Palmer method was to laugh at it. And listening to my grandmother telling it, making up bits as she went along about the imaginary Mr. Palmer who was so set on exercising the underside of children's forearms, I had to laugh again. We all laughed until we were laughed out.

My grandmother turned serious. "You can't move your fingers at all?" she asked, as if she might not have heard right the first time.

"Not at all."

My grandmother shook her head. "They must be preparing you for a crippled old age." She leaned down to comfort Josh. "Sh, sh, sh," she said, smoothing out his feathers. "It's all right, Josh. It's all over. You don't know how funny the world can be, do you? Maybe even a little crazy. There are times when people just *have* to laugh."

"Times when they have to eat too," my grandfather added. "What are we having?"

My grandmother said she'd fixed apple dumplings, and together the three of us walked to the house. Past the cabbages and beans, down the path lined with gold and orange chrysanthemums. We stopped to admire the grapes, dangling in heavy clusters from the vines, fat and purple.

Then I ran ahead to put the plates on the table.

When my mother and father arrived in China in 1913, China had been a republic with a president for only a year. For thousands of years before this, China had been ruled by emperors and empresses who had tried to seal China off from the rest of the world. Early in the nineteenth century, however, Western nations had gradually been exerting their power and forcing their way into the country. In a series of "unequal" treaties, the foreign nations gained "concessions" in which Western law was practiced and Western police kept order; they put gunboats on the rivers to protect the interests of Western merchants. By 1907 there were thousands of foreign businessmen and foreign missionaries in China (3500 Protestant missionaries alone).

Eventually the Chinese rebelled not only against this Western imposition but against their own internal system which served a ruling class at the expense of millions of farmers and laborers. The leader of the revolutionary movement was a Chinese Christian by the name of Sun Yat-sen who had been educated in both Chinese and British schools. "China is being transformed everywhere," he wrote, "into a colony of foreign powers." Sun Yat-sen was in America when the revolution actually broke out on October 10, 1911, in Wuchang, across the river from Hankow. Sun went back to China and was sworn in as president of the

Republic of China on January 1, 1912. But he needed military help to back up his government, so he consented to an agreement with Yuan Shih-k'ai, a military leader in the imperial army. If Yuan completed the overthrow of the old imperial government, Yuan could be president of the new republic.

The trouble was that Yuan Shih-k'ai did not share Sun Yat-sen's ideas for a democratic China. Once he became president, he was interested only in power; he even tried to get himself elected emperor. When he died on June 6, 1916, the country was no further ahead than it had been in 1912.

While warlords fought back and forth, Sun Yat-sen made another attempt at national unity. Although he was head of the Nationalist party, he still did not have the military support he needed to get rid of the warlords and do away with the special privileges of the foreigners. "The only country that shows any sign of helping us," he wrote, "is the Soviet Government of Russia." Beginning in September 1922, he allowed Chinese Communists to join his party, and the following year the Russians began sending advisers to China. Later they sent arms. Sun himself was not a Communist and had he lived, he might have been able to unite China in the way he wanted. Unfortunately, Sun Yat-sen died on March 12, 1925, and was later succeeded by Chiang Kai-shek as party leader. By August 1926, Chiang had marched the National Revolutionary Army north, gathering warlords on the way, and was at the Yangtse River.

Meanwhile Hankow, an industrial city, had become a central point for strikes, agitation, and anti-foreign demonstrations. Behind the scenes Mao Tse-tung was organizing peasants for a Communist uprising, but

Chiang was against the idea of peasants taking violent action against their landlords. In order to ensure a united China, Chiang believed he had to make deals with Chinese capitalists, with members of China's underworld, and with foreigners who believed that with Chiang in charge, they could continue business as usual. He eliminated Communists from his party and in April 1927 (after the Nanking Incident), he set up his own government in Nanking. Foreign nations recognized this as the legal government of China. By August the Russians had left China and Mao Tse-tung and his small band of followers were hiding in the hills.

It was during this turbulent period of transition that I was in China. Struggle and civil war (interrupted by a war with Japan) continued for twenty-two years before Mao Tse-tung defeated Chiang Kai-shek and established the People's Republic of China. Chiang, with remnants of his army and many of his followers, took refuge on the island of Taiwan, where they continued a government which they claimed was still the government of all China. America recognized that government as the government of China until December 1978, although it had lost its seat in the United Nations in 1971.

Dear Grandma.

Thank you so much for the petticoat. It is lovely. The thing that I think is nice about it is that it is so much like a grown ups petticoat. Everything was perfectly beautiful. Thank Aunt Margaret and aunt Etta please for the ring. I am wearing it now. And please thank Aunt Margaret for the pocket book. I am so proud of it, that when I take it out with me everyone notices me and says. What a pretty pocket book where did you get it? Shall I name the presents I got? Fountain pen, Stamp album. (from mother) Dolls furniture (from Daddy) lovely invitations cards. (aunt maud) Black Coat, (aunt Maud,) album, Paper, paper, beads, little Angel cake cookers, Book of furniture. Pink silk cloth, Brown Satin, White, rubber apron (cousin Margaret,) my petticoat, pocket book. Gag, 1 book, 2 book, 3 book, Dolls clothes, gold pail, pocket book gold bracelet, stocking full of things, dolls teaset, 1 candy box, 2 candy box, hankerchiefs (galore,) shawl, skipping rope, 1926 Good day Diary.

With loads of
Love
Your Granddaughter

Jean Guthrie.

1925 Christmas letter from Jean to her grandmother

Top: Jean at age ten
Bottom: Jean's class at the Hankow British School.
Ian Forbes is second from right. (Jean was absent that day.)

Top: The Hulls' house
Bottom left: Lin Nai-Nai
Bottom right: Climbing a tree at Andrea's house

Top: Swinging at Andrea's house
Bottom: Andrea and small friend

Top: Jean's father
Bottom: Jean's mother

Summer at Peitaiho

Opposite page
Top: Junk on Yangtse River
Middle: The Bund
Bottom: Y.M.C.A. building

Top: Marketplace
Bottom: Jean's mother in a rickshaw

Buildings bombed in Wuchang

Top: Steamers anchored at Hankow
Bottom: Jean

Jean's grandparents